SUSTAIN

Jo Barrett

SUSTAIN

Groundbreaking recipes and skills
that could save the planet

Hardie Grant

BOOKS

To my brothers Aidan and Michael.
You will always be smarter, cooler and older than me.

And my wonderful parents,
I couldn't have asked for better.

Contents

Foreword **9**

The future of food **11**

Introduction **13**

Seasonality and scale **14**

Connecting to a sustainable food system **17**

Why should you trust me? **18**

Before you get started **21**

Setting up **22**

A bit more about me **25**

How to use this book **27**

The recipe matrix **28**

The impacts **30**

1 **Sprout balls with cashew and fenugreek** 33

2 **Glazed mushroom skewers** 41

3 **Cumin wallaby skewers with garlic yoghurt** 49

4 **Roasted marrow bones with compound butter on sourdough** 55

5 **Yabbie dumplings with nasturtium and chilli oil** 67

6 **Barramundi and sorghum tostadas with pickled jalapeños and green coriander seeds** 75

7 **Stuffed potato cakes with tomato–chilli relish** 83

8 **Freshly milled flatbread with 'nduja and sweet onion** 91

9 **Zucchini and fermented bean rice cakes** 99

10 **Garden bread** 107

11 **Avocado salsa with parsley-seed dressing and eggs on toast** 113

12 Broccoli, buckwheat and seaweed salad 119

13 Smoked trout with celeriac and spring onion remoulade 127

14 Sauerkraut soup with fromage blanc 137

15 Rooster broth with buckwheat noodles and pickled mushrooms 145

16 Fried sardines with roasted almonds, skordalia and parsley salad 153

17 Murray cod with fennel salad and marinated vegetable dressing 159

18 Venison and red wine pie 167

19 Stuffed rainbow chard with olives, capers and preserved lemon in tomato sugo 175

20 Red pepper pasta 183

21 Sprout risotto 191

22 Roast potatoes with macadamia pesto 197

23 Brussels sprouts and bacon with mushroom XO 205

24 Ultimate seed mix 213

25 Tigernut cake with preserved quince 219

26 Layered lemon with granita, honey and yuzu curd 227

27 Plum galette with caccio ricotta 235

28 Sponge cake with rhubarb and lemon myrtle jam 245

29 Whole orange parfait with citrus–butter sauce 253

30 Honey–miso caramel 261

Acknowledgements **267**

Index **268**

Foreword

By Dani Valent

I remember the first time I had a proper chat with Jo Barrett. It was at Oakridge Wines in 2017, and I'd just rounded off a lovely, thought-provoking Yarra Valley lunch by eating her 'compost dessert'. If that sounds a little pongy and dodgy, let me assure you it wasn't. Shiraz lees were refashioned into a purple granita, grapefruit peel was turned into a citrus paste, ice cream was flavoured with coriander stems and roots, and shards of meringue – made with leftover egg whites – added height and crunch to a dish that hit all the right notes: pretty, sweet, tart, textural, playful and surprising.

There were two other aspects that struck me, qualities I've come to realise are Jo Barrett hallmarks: this was a dessert with purpose and meaning. The gorgeous plate of food wasn't just there to be eaten, it also had messages. 'Waste is a disconnection from consequence and a failure of imagination,' it was saying. And also, 'Here's a solution.' That's Jo: apprehending a problem and optimistically demonstrating a fix that also happens to be delicious.

We chatted in the Oakridge wine library; except it wasn't a wine library. Jo had taken her hand-cranked grain mill into this little bottle-lined chamber and she milled wheat there every day before preparing bread and pastries for the restaurant. I turned the wheel a few times, felt the power of the machine in the crunch and give of the grain and sensed the extraordinary intention that was behind this endeavour. Jo's eyes were shining. Around us, the venerable Oakridge bottles, special enough to make it into the library, were coated in a fine layer of flour.

I followed this interesting, compelling chef as she progressed. There were her gob-smacking efforts at the 'dessert Olympics' in Milan, where she built a metre-tall sugar-sculpted emu for the judges. Of course, there was futurefoodsystem, the eco-house and life experiment that stood in the centre of Melbourne for a year, transforming ideas about what sustainable living and eating might really look like. There were the Have A Go lockdown booklets, which encouraged people to bake croissants and make cheese. And along the way, knife making, fly fishing, diving, fire cooking, a slew of other projects unleashed with a fearless humility.

That Jo Barrett would write a book doesn't surprise me. It is obvious, really. She has so much to say. She is practical. She is a sharer. She's obsessed with learning, information, method, doing, enacting and bringing into being. If I heard her say one day, 'Everest was there so I climbed it,' it wouldn't be that shocking, though I would be startled if she didn't then speak about the wild herbs growing at altitude.

Even so, this book did surprise me. Don't tell Jo, but I'll admit I was a tiny bit sceptical at first. Can you really expect everyday home cooks to swap beef for wallaby, make their own miso and nixtamalise sorghum? I started reading the recipes and before I knew it, I had gone to the spice drawer, dug out some fenugreek seeds and preserved them in vinegar, just like on page 39. This is the Jo Barrett Effect. I see sprouted grain balls in my future and – even better – it means the future will be a tiny bit better.

Just like Jo, this book is ambitious, clever and joyful. It's also infused with a sense of what's possible for all of us.

The future of food

By Joost Bakker

I was lucky to meet Jo when she worked for me at the Greenhouse in 2012. The pop-up restaurant on Melbourne's Yarra River was like a magnet pulling brilliant, like-minded people together, all sharing a belief that we could do more and be better. Her enthusiasm, hard work and no bullshit approach was refreshing, and we quickly created a bond. Jo's great attribute is her constant desire to learn. She is forever digging deeper to understand almost everything, exploring the world's most complex problems with unrelenting determination.

Not long after meeting Jo, I became frustrated with the lack of awareness around food and how its many broken systems are destroying the world that I love. While we all hold unlimited access to information in our hands, we still lose the equivalent of 27 soccer fields of biodiverse forest every minute. At our current rate of extraction, the world's oceans will have no fish at all by 2048. Waste is a human thing, and no other species 'creates' waste.

Jo and I would often discuss these issues, and she was forever positive with a strong belief that solutions do exist. The idea of creating another Greenhouse manifested, and by 2020 we were ready to launch futurefoodsystem, a fully operational house in Federation Square in the middle of the city (pictured left), highlighting problems and showing solutions. The aim was to grow delicious, nourishing food using the world's most abundant waste at its source and create a productive building that was a zero waste ecosystem.

Futurefoodsystem was meant to simply be Jo and her then-partner Matt's home while they went to work and lived normal lives, showing that busy people can have productive spaces, but we embarked on this project at an unprecedented time of uncertainty. Doing such a public project during a global pandemic forced us to be creative, and suddenly we had a global audience who were stuck in their homes looking at what we created on laptops and smartphones.

My favourite memories are that we all had a sense of purpose and drive; we felt lucky that we had this project to work on while the rest of the world was shut down. For all involved we look back on this time as being incredibly creative, fertile ground for change. We showed a food system that was inspired by Indigenous Australians: resilient, complex, diverse, nourishing and delicious. Jo's enthusiasm for all facets of this project from construction to execution is what really made this project succeed. It made it truly feel like a home. I hope it will be the home of the future.

What I especially love about this book is the celebration of ingredients that can restore and rebalance our environment, ingredients like sorghum, yabbies and the humble tiger nut that has nourished humanity for over 2 million years. At futurefoodsystem Jo embraced this ingredient and created some of the most memorable dishes I have ever eaten, especially the cake featured in this book! I believe this and the other recipes in *Sustain* can inspire you to think and cook more sustainably in your kitchen.

Introduction

HOW DO YOU EAT AN ELEPHANT? ONE BITE AT A TIME!

The oft-used quote above (attributed to a few authors) is funny and ideal to explain the aim of this cookbook. Firstly, you're not alone if you're feeling overwhelmed with the whole concept of sustainable cooking and eating. You might feel cynical when I suggest that what you choose to put in your mouth can have a sustainable impact on our Earth. Let me share my theory of subtle impacts, which won't ask you to be a vegan, gluten free or an 'anything'. You will not have to join a cult, in fact just the opposite. This way of consuming is asking you to think for yourself.

Sustain is a manual of ideas to consider, practices to adopt and techniques to learn. Each bite-sized chunk you take will have a subtle impact on you and the Earth over time. When you make these choices, you create a demand for sustainable produce, which means you're helping to create a market for the producer who uses sustainable methods and respects the seasons.

Why this, why now?

We've heard it all before: the climate crisis is happening. Those words evoke feelings of anxiety, guilt and grief, and populations across the globe are feeling the pain of this existential threat. We've missed the crossroad and we're heading down the wrong track. Again. Bitter disappointment and fear, but there's only one way back: a U-turn. A challenging manoeuvre that needs awareness of your surroundings and skill.

What we may not realise is that food is a major culprit. The current food system (production, transportation, consumption and huge amounts of waste) is having a disastrous effect on the natural environment.

These impacts are personal too. Even the simplest act of supermarket shopping can induce choice paralysis. How do we know what food is good for our bodies and the planet? How did we get to this point? More importantly, how do we move on from here to better nutrition, health and a thriving, balanced ecosystem? And, can it be delicious too?

Yes, it can! If food is the problem, the good news is food can also be the solution. It keeps us alive, brings us together, can change our mood, heal our bodies and save our planet. As my grandad would say, 'We all eat.' We all have the opportunity to make positive change by valuing food; the time spent producing it, preparing it and eating it. Cooking skills can be the handbrake on destructive food production, over-fishing, excess packaging, poor health and food waste, AND be an accelerator to awareness, confidence, creativity and satisfaction. We can shun foods that wreak havoc on our ecosystems and vote with our knife and fork, and more specifically, our wallet.

Cooking starts from the ground up. Our nutrition depends on what plants absorb from the soil. When we eat animals, the same principle applies, but we are higher up the food chain.

Two factors to consider are seasonality and scale.

Seasonality and scale

Natural growth is seasonal. When we cook with ingredients from the season when they're at their prime, they are abundant, nutritionally rich, full-flavoured and textured, and require fewer inputs, because that's the way nature intended. Cooking and consuming out of season is costly to the consumer, the producer and the environment, as it requires more infrastructure and resources.

Large scale farming comes with inherent risk. Creating monocultures replaces essential biodiversity, making them less resilient to pests and disease. This usually manifests in the use of chemicals to control these problems. Both monocultures and chemical use deplete the soil quality and integrity.

I can almost hear your thoughts, and I've actually heard your questions. 'What can I do about this?', 'I'm only one person!', 'I don't know where to start' and 'I'm not a farmer.' Cooking local, seasonal produce is the answer. This doesn't mean you need to live in a rural setting or on a farm. You don't need to keep chickens and you don't even need to grow your own produce. Over 50 per cent of our population currently lives in urban cities, and it's unrealistic to think that most of us will drop-shop and pick up a shovel. Yet we can still save the planet from our kitchen benches. Individual action can have a ripple effect.

Connecting to a sustainable food system

MAKE SURE YOU READ THIS BIT

If you buy a capsicum (bell pepper) out of season, the capsicum requires more energy and resources to grow because the farmer needs to replicate the ideal growing conditions. If a farmer is growing only capsicums in a crop (monoculture) they become vulnerable. One pest or disease could wipe out the whole lot.

If I were a farmer, I would want to secure my crop, so I can understand why farmers spray crops to protect their livelihoods.

Instead, if you go to a farmers' market and only buy what's in season, there are many benefits to the environment. Not only are you supporting local producers and positive agricultural practices (they will not be as reliant on pesticides to secure their crops), you are also reducing waste and food miles.

UNSUSTAINABLE

Buy capsicum out of season

If farmer growing only capsicums (monoculture), the crop may become vulnerable to pest/disease

Requires more energy and resources to grow

SUSTAINABLE

Buy capsicum in season at farmers' market

Support local producers and positive agricultural practices

Take pressure off farmers

Reduce waste and food miles by purchasing whole local ingredients in minimal or no packaging

You begin to appreciate the patterns of seasonal abundance and capture it with forms of food preservation

You build a pantry that you can use year-round

You're connected to a more sustainable food system

Why should you trust me?

I'm not a climate scientist; I'm a chef. I hear and read about the crisis probably from the same sources as you: the internet, socials, TV, books, peers, political debate, etc. The intensity and increasing frequency of the discussion tells me it's real. You can dispute the details, but it's impossible to ignore the evidence. My personal and professional experiences also inform my understanding of what's happening, and I trust myself.

Dedicating my career to food was easy, but witnessing harmful agricultural practices, lazy, short-cut kitchen habits and excessive waste was not. You may have wondered about the plethora of cooking shows on our screens recently, showing competent chefs hunting, fishing and foraging, then cooking over coals in the wilderness. Why? Cooks are the 'canary in the coal mine'. We're the link between producer and consumer. Chefs are championing change: zero waste restaurants, nose-to-tail dishes from farm-to-plate establishments.

Skills enable us to cook like this, and in days gone by, traditional methods were employed in home kitchens too. I've spent a lifetime collecting skills. I'm a control freak, too proud to not know. It's a deep dive – a never-ending quest for the why and how. As I shaped thousands of loaves and croissants at Tivoli Road Bakery, my food philosophy was also being shaped. The provenance of food became paramount, and its culinary value was literally 'in my hands'.

We were truly at the mercy of the elements at Oakridge Winery, where a large kitchen garden complemented the award-winning vineyard and the menu strictly represented our success as amateur growers.

Joost Bakker's futurefoodsystem clarified any doubt I had about sustainable cooking. It's eminently possible. With an 87 square metre (936 square feet) footprint, this productive, off-grid, zero waste, non-toxic building in Melbourne's Federation Square sustained its inhabitants – Matt Stone and myself – and diners with over 200 species of edible plants and animals. If we could grow it on or in the urban house, then it was on the menu. No cow meant no meat or dairy, and there was no refined sugar or flour for baking.

I soon learnt constraint equalled creativity, and our collective cooking skills saved us. For the first time, I really realised that we belonged to an ecosystem and that we hold responsibilities in that system. It was at futurefoodsystem that I met people just like you and me. Their burning question was always, 'Where do I start?' This book is my response.

Share food and the message. We can make the U-turn for a better world.

Before you get started

Clean your equipment: two ways to sterilise

Clean, sterile equipment is essential for successful and prolonged food preserving. Bacteria thrive in moist, temperate, food-rich environments. Food stored in jars in these conditions creates an ideal ecosystem for good and bad bacteria growth. It's our role as the food preserver to control the environment for beneficial bacteria to thrive, so that we can avoid the nasties. Harmful bacteria cause food spoilage, reduce shelf life, make food unpalatable and can lead to food poisoning. They can appear as colourful moulds, smell astringent or overly funky and taste bitter, but they can also be undetectable. That's the scary bit.

There are simple steps to reduce the risk of this happening. Practice good personal hygiene by washing your hands, work cleanly to prevent cross contamination and use clean, sterilised equipment.

For general cooking utensils, such as spoons, ladles, thermometers, etc.:

Wash the equipment in hot soapy water and rinse. Fill a pot with water and bring it to the boil. Submerge the equipment into boiling water for one minute then place it on a clean tea towel to dry.

An efficient way to sterilise glass jars:

Preheat the oven to 110°C (230°F) and heat the clean jars for 20 minutes. Remove them from the oven and allow them to cool. Place the clean jar lids in boiling water for 5 minutes.

The aim of each method is to kill any potential bacteria with heat over time. This gives you a 'clean slate' and allows for effective and safe preserving.

The salt equation: calculating with percentages

Many of the recipes in this book require a percentage of salt based on the weight of another ingredient. Below is the formula for how to calculate this, but if maths isn't your strong point or you prefer to leave the calculator in the drawer, you can do like we often do in the kitchen and simply ask your smartphone.

$$\frac{\text{Weight in g/oz (or ml/fl oz)} \times \text{percentage of salt}}{100}$$

$$\text{E.g.} \frac{250 \text{ g/9 oz cabbage} \times 2\% \text{ salt}}{100}$$

$$= 5 \text{ g/⅛ oz salt}$$

Setting up

THESE ARE MY GO-TO ITEMS FOR THE KITCHEN

Digital scales and digital thermometers
These take out the guess work. Accuracy is often key to achieving consistent results. Weigh and measure as required.

Muslin and beeswax wraps
I don't use cling wrap. I use muslin for cheese making but also for wrapping cut vegetables, cheeses and herbs. Beeswax wraps are another alternative to cling wrap.

Jars
Keep a range of jars in all shapes and sizes. They're essential for successful preserving. Use wide-mouthed jars for fruit, bottles for sauces and smaller options for jams.

Cheese measuring spoons
Some recipes, such as cheesemaking, require very small but accurate measurements, such as $1/5$ of $1/4$ teaspoon. Cheese measuring spoons, which use the measurements drop, smidgen, pinch, dash and tad, will be required for these recipes.

Airtight containers
To store ingredients, prolong shelf life and reduce food waste.

Heavy based pots
Find some that are large enough to make big batches of sauce and jam to increase efficiency.

Large mixing bowl
I always think I won't need a large mixing bowl at home until it comes to making sauerkraut or salting vegetables.

Salt
The number one ingredient for fermenting, curing and most forms of preserving. I use salt flakes and fine salt harvested from salt flats or sea water for seasoning and preserving. I want them as natural as possible for their mineral content and natural bacteria.

Olive oil
This oil has antibacterial qualities and is a natural preserver. Use an olive oil that has a subtle flavour and isn't overly fruity, so it can be used for applications from salad dressings to marinades.

Grapeseed oil
This oil has little flavour and is ideal for cooking at high temperatures and carrying flavour.

Vinegar
This ingredient is essential for pickling, preserving and enhancing flavour. I love experimenting with different vinegars. Pantry staples are apple cider, brown rice, white and red wine vinegar.

Honey
Where possible, I use honey instead of refined sugar. It's natural, has antibacterial properties and preserves. Honey has a distinct flavour, so it doesn't always work as a substitute for sugar.

Sugar
This is another key preserving ingredient. It prevents bacterial growth and enhances flavour. I use raw or caster sugar where appropriate.

A note on produce
Always use the best. Buy organic. Support local. Stick to the seasons.

A bit more about me

Little kids have big dreams. A favourite question that adults ask them is, 'What would you like to do when you grow up?' Adults do this on a regular basis, probably because a pre-schooler's response is usually so beguiling and free from self-conscious judgement. A visit to the kindergarten by the local fire brigade produces aspiring fire fighters. Young kids want to be that kindly doctor who helped them to get better when they were really sick. Footage of elite gymnasts has them heading to the 'limpics' to win a gold medal. If you read them a moving or adventurous story, then they insist that they're going to write a book one day. So, I laugh with amazement that I achieved these last two ambitions.

Well, sort of. I didn't win a gold medal when I represented Australia at the World Pastry Championships in Milan, but I felt incredibly proud of my 1.5 metre emu entirely constructed from sugar when I carried it gingerly to the judges' table. It took two years of preparation to get to a destination that's globally considered the culinary Olympics of all things pastry. Just like at other world competitions, there were crowds, flags, big band fanfare and enormous screens broadcasting all the epic triumphs and devastating failures. And now you're reading my book, *Sustain*. Here's the thing. I believed I would write a cookbook, but I didn't think that it would be about sustainability. My editor suggested that I tell something about my philosophy and how I got to this point, but I'll have to go back to those early days when my imagination was as big as yours once was.

When I was two years old, our family moved to an idyllic one-acre block that was heavily treed and unfenced. It was atypical of its pretentious outer Melbourne suburb, and a local creek babbled along near the bottom of our long gravel driveway. Adjacent to our boundaries lived some neighbours who had been friends for decades and shared a huge productive garden.

My idol, John, was a gruff, sixty-something pharmacist by day, who had no plans to ever retire. He smoked incessantly and brewed his own beer in a back shed. He maintained a beautiful rose garden and was respected by his wife, kids and grandkids. He let me burn sticks in a giant brick incinerator and gave me a glass of ginger beer poured from dusty bottles (also in the shed) when I helped in the veggie garden on the weekends. When I was four, I told him that I was going to be a chef. Shortly after, he turned out 20 little rolling pins on his lathe for me to take to kindergarten. You can see how it happens; I was destined and determined to be a chef.

I didn't consider myself an academic at school, so I was surprised when I performed well. However, I still bypassed uni and headed straight for the kitchen. Delacy's was a small bistro with a daytime clientele of city lawyers and their colleagues, and I loved starting my apprenticeship there. Right from day one, I had responsibilities and felt like part of a team. I was filleting fish, making sauces and petit fours, maintaining an organised service fridge and, of course, washing lots of dishes. The head chef, Andrew Irwin, trusted me with real tasks, which set me up with a solid foundation.

A trip to Canada on a culinary scholarship furthered my interest in traditional cooking techniques, such as charcuterie, table-side carving and ice sculpting! I was now part of a large, formal kitchen brigade. I knew it was a serious deal when all staff were expected at wine training, and our chef uniforms were laundered professionally. We got to wear big hats. It was puzzling, though, to wash frisée lettuce when it was -20°C (-4°F) and snowing outside ... that sat somewhere in my subconscious.

For a time, I muddled about in a few different kitchen settings with increasing pressure and responsibilities. But I always avoided pastry. My belief about being a competent head chef in all areas pushed me directly into a patisserie course when I joined the opening team at Movida/Tivoli Road Bakery with Michael James. This experience was a steep learning curve that changed my thinking momentously. Here, I learnt about the process of learning, specifically learning without fear.

My mum was a P.E. teacher and was always banging on about the 'four stages of competence'. It does my head in, but you know what they say: 'The apple doesn't fall far from the tree'. I like good results – every time! So, when I tackled sourdough bread at the bakery, it wasn't as straightforward as I expected it to be; it wasn't enough to just follow a recipe.

So, let me introduce you to the four stages of competence, credited to Gordon Training International by its employee Noel Burch in the 1970s.

Stage 1
Unconscious incompetence = you don't know what you don't know (most of us start here with a new task).

Stage 2
Conscious incompetence = you know what you don't know (often overwhelming).

Stage 3
Conscious competence = you know that you can do it now (need for concentration).

Stage 4
Unconscious competence = you can do it without thinking about it (it's become second nature, so you need to be aware of this when you're training someone else but it also gives you freedom to be creative).

I started at Movida Bakery at stage 1. I really didn't know what I was doing. Sure, I could follow recipes and produce goods under instruction, but I couldn't troubleshoot in the same way that I had been able to in previous kitchens. As soon as one variable changed, I was stuck. It was so frustrating not knowing. Thankfully my endless stream of questions was met with Michael's inexhaustible patience and knowledge. Over time and much repetition, I became competent but also aware that no matter how consistent my technique was, there were still inconsistencies in the loaves. This was a defining moment. There was another deeper layer to consider. The provenance of the grain. I realised that even before I laid hands on the flour, its qualities were determined by how and where it was grown, stored and transported. This spurred me on to ask and investigate. I began to consider the provenance of all other ingredients. What was the point of pursuing excellent technique if the produce was inferior, unseasonal or unethical with unpredictable qualities. Chefs say it all the time – good cooking starts with good produce.

My next career progressions were in partnership with the formidable team of Joost Bakker and Matt Stone, who share similar ideals of zero waste and closed-loop cooking. They were committed and fearless in their convictions, resulting in ground-breaking projects, including Greenhouse, Silo, Brothl and, ultimately, futurefoodsystem. Matt and I were pleased to be able to demonstrate these principles over five years at award winning Oakridge Winery. Matt's confidence to not falter from ethical cooking – even when faced with guests' demands and the expected 'norm' – was inspiring and gave me a lot of confidence. Together we were able to support each other and it was a very creative time of research, testing and skill building. I feel really proud of what we achieved at Oakridge.

There are so many components of cooking and being a chef that I love. The endless learning is the best part, and it wasn't until writing this book that I realised I've spent my career gathering skills. When I'm under pressure, the freedom and creativity I feel as a result of having these skills to draw on is extraordinary – perhaps this is how ballet dancers and opera singers feel when they are performing. Complete contentment and unconscious competence.

How to use this book

Sustain is a compilation of 30 dishes that you can make any day of the week, and each dish is prepared from component recipes. You can buy these components from a store, or you can make the components yourself by following the skill builder recipes.

Mastering these techniques will give you knowledge and confidence. You'll learn the skills to make informed decisions, use seasonal produce, minimise waste and produce healthy, delicious food. In essence, you'll be able to live a more sustainable life through food and the way you eat.

I haven't reinvented the wheel, as these skills are centuries old; we've just lost touch with what's possible and practical. Once you understand how simple these processes really are, then you can enjoy an unexpected gift of lemons, make a thrifty choice of cabbage over unseasonal lettuce, and perhaps impress your friends with a meal made from scratch! You'll develop the skills to cook with what's available.

To live and cook like this might require a mind shift. Ideally, you'll build a pantry, preserve, eat seasonally and get creative. Be patient with yourself. You don't need to attempt all the skills at once. Quality components are readily available from organic and specialty stores, online and at markets – just buy them until you're ready to have a go at the skill builder recipes.

The recipe matrix

Cook the following DISHES with these RECIPES to learn various SKILLS
and make a positive IMPACT

DISHES	RECIPES	SKILLS	IMPACT
Sprout balls with cashew and fenugreek	Sprout balls Sprouting pulses Aged fenugreek Cashew and fenugreek cream	Making nut cream Preserving in vinegar Sprouting pulses	Add nutrients Vegan Gluten free Pantry staples
Glazed mushroom skewers	Mushroom skewers Mushroom glaze Mushroom garum Koji rice	Advanced fermenting	Adds nutrients Zero waste Pantry staples
Cumin wallaby skewers with garlic yoghurt	Wallaby skewers Cumin spice mix Garlic yoghurt Yoghurt	Making yoghurt	Sustainable proteins Adds nutrients
Roasted marrow bones with compound butter on sourdough	Marrow bones Butter Compound butter Cultured butter Sourdough bread starter Sourdough bread	Brining Making butter Making a sourdough starter Sourdough baking	Alternative ingredients Zero waste
Yabbie dumplings with nasturtium and chilli oil	Yabbie dumplings Chilli oil	Preserving	Sustainable proteins Pantry staples Gluten free
Barramundi and sorghum tostadas with pickled jalapeños and green coriander seeds	Barramundi tostadas Green coriander seeds Pickled jalapeños Sorghum tostadas	Nixtamalisation	Alternative ingredients Pantry staples Capture abundance
Stuffed potato cakes with tomato–chilli relish	Potato cakes Tomato–chilli relish	Preserving	Zero waste Captures abundance Pantry staples
Freshly milled flatbread with 'nduja and sweet onion	Flatbread Sweet onion 'Nduja Milling grains	Baking Charcuterie Milling grains	Alternative ingredients
Zucchini and fermented bean rice cakes	Rice cakes Batter Fermented beans	Basic fermenting	Capture abundance Pantry staples
Garden bread	Garden bread Pumpkin puree	Gluten-free baking	Zero waste Gluten free
Avocado salsa with parsley-seed dressing and eggs on toast	Fried eggs and salsa Parsley seed dressing Herb flower and seed oil	Preserving	Alternative ingredients Pantry staples
Broccoli, buckwheat and seaweed salad	Broccoli and buckwheat salad Macadamia milk Diced dressing	Nut milks Preserving	Alternative ingredients Vegan Pantry staples
Smoked trout with celeriac and spring onion remoulade	Smoked trout with remoulade Salt cure Aioli Confit garlic	Preserving	Alternative ingredients Pantry staples Capture abundance
Sauerkraut soup with fromage blanc	Sauerkraut soup Sauerkraut Fromage blanc	Basic fermenting Cheese making	Capture abundance Add nutrients

DISHES	RECIPES	SKILLS	IMPACT
Rooster broth with buckwheat noodles and pickled mushrooms	Rooster broth with noodles Rooster bone broth Pickled mushrooms Pickling liquid Buckwheat noodles	Noodle making Pickling Bone broth	Alternative ingredients Capture abundance Zero waste
Fried sardines with roasted almonds, skordalia and parsley salad	Fried sardines Skordalia Parsley salad		Gluten free
Murray cod with fennel salad and marinated vegetable dressing	Murray cod Fennel salad Marinated vegetable dressing Preserved vegetables Red wine vinegar	Preserving in oil Making vinegar	Sustainable proteins Captures abundance Pantry staples
Venison and red wine pie	Venison pie Rough puff pastry	Pie making	Sustainable proteins
Stuffed rainbow chard with olives, capers and preserved lemon in tomato sugo	Stuffed rainbow chard Tomato sugo Preserved lemons	Preserving	Captures abundance Pantry staple
Red pepper pasta	Red pepper pasta Rye pasta Fermented red peppers	Basic fermenting Pasta making	Captures abundance
Sprout risotto	Sprout risotto Spinach puree Cashew cream	Making nut creams Sprouting grains	Vegan
Roast potatoes with macadamia pesto	Roast potatoes Macadamia pesto	Preserving	Captures abundance
Brussels sprouts and bacon with mushroom XO	Brussels sprouts and bacon Mushroom XO Fermented chilli Bacon Cure	Preserving Basic fermenting Curing Charcuterie	Captures abundance Pantry staples
Ultimate seed mix	Seed mix		Vegan
Tigernut cake with preserved quince	Tigernut cake Honey-cooked quinces	Preserving	Pantry staples Alternative ingredients Gluten free Captures abundance
Layered lemon with granita, honey and yuzu curd	Layered lemons Lemon granita Yuzu curd Flavoured citrus oil	Preserving	Captures abundance Pantry staples
Plum galette with caccio ricotta	Galette pastry Bottled plums Caccio ricotta	Making pastry Preserving Cheese making	Captures abundance Pantry staples
Sponge cake with rhubarb and lemon myrtle jam	Sponge cake Rhubarb and lemon myrtle jam	Technical baking Preserving	Captures abundance Pantry staples Alternative ingredients
Whole orange parfait with citrus–butter sauce	Parfait Orange puree Citrus–butter sauce Candied fennel seeds	Parfait Preserving	Captures abundance Pantry staples
Honey-miso caramel	Honey-miso caramel Miso	Advanced fermenting	Pantry staples

The impacts

HOW THE RECIPES IN THIS BOOK CAN HELP YOU MAKE A DIFFERENCE

Add nutrients

A nutrient is a substance used by an organism to survive, grow and reproduce, and we need a range of nutrients to ensure that we stay alive and function well. Over time, we have reduced the variety of fruits, vegetables and herbs in our diet. This is obvious in the fresh food area at the supermarket, where there is an abundance of produce but not much variety. Heirloom species are scarce on the shelves, even though they offer nutritional diversity. Extracting the most nutrients from an ingredient is crucial to living a healthy life, and we can increase this nutritional diversity by eating a broad range of ingredients and by fermenting and activating (sprouting). We feel nourished and satisfied eating nutrient-dense food, and we don't need to eat as much.

Vegan

Ruminant animals produce methane, which is a hazardous air pollutant and powerful greenhouse gas. By replacing beef and lamb with plant-based alternatives that have similar nutritional value, we can reduce the amount of methane released into the atmosphere.

Gluten free

Gluten-free recipes are essential for people with gluten intolerance and gluten sensitivity to prevent sickness. For others who are not afflicted with these conditions, it's not about removing wheat from your diet; it's more relevant to avoid heavily refined wheat that is nutritionally deficient. Wholegrains supply a source of fibre that's important for digestion, and when we eat alternative grain options (which are often cultivated for crop rotation), we reduce the pressure for increased wheat production.

Zero waste

If we all spent some time growing produce, we would begin to understand the effort and resources that are expended with food production. We might think twice about wasting food and we could even save some money. When organic material goes into landfill instead of being composted, it doesn't break down effectively, and the waste produces methane, which is worse than carbon dioxide. According to OzHarvest and the World Resources Institute, 'Wasting food is worse than total emissions from flying (1.9%), plastic production (3.8%) and oil extraction (3.8%).' Using all parts of an ingredient and finding multiple uses for biproducts can have a profoundly positive impact. For example, bone broth can be a secondary use for bones.

Alternative ingredients

There are many parts of plants and animals that are often discarded that could be used in our kitchens, and these can provide nutritional value that is equal to or sometimes higher than that of the more popular cuts. Some examples are pork back fat, bone marrow, green seeds from herbs and leafy tops of root vegetables.

Pantry staples

Stocking your pantry with your own preserved ingredients is a powerful way to positively impact the food system and save money. You're using seasonal produce when it's abundant, full-flavoured and at its best price. You also reduce the need for packaging and gain knowledge and control over the preserving process. Having a collection of preserves at hand to use at any time of the year means fewer trips to the shops. For me, that's a good thing.

Sustainable proteins

Plants and animals thrive in their natural habitat. Evolution selects species that suit the prevailing weather patterns, available resources and terrain. The biome constantly strives for balance. When we introduce exotic plants and animals, it can disturb this natural order. The introduced plant or animal may have different resource requirements, making heavier demands on feed and water. They may present a higher risk of pest and disease to an ecosystem, which creates an imperative to treat with pesticides and antibiotics or employ other protective interventions. This is how we currently provide food for the world's populations and enjoy unbridled access to exotic and unseasonal ingredients, but there's a huge cost to the Earth's environment and biodiversity for this convenience. When we consciously choose to consume naturally occurring ingredients, we're promoting food sources that are free-range and organic, with little or no farming interventions. Tasty and ethical.

Preserving

Preserving uses various techniques to maintain food quality and prevent food from spoiling. This extends the item's shelf life, enhances its flavour and texture, and adds nutritional value. Techniques like fermentation, pickling, curing, bottling, drying and freezing are forms of food preservation.

Capture abundance

The skills of preserving a glut of produce prevent food waste and support seasonal growing for farmers. In Australia, nearly half of all vegetables grown are wasted. Behind this mountain of waste produce sits a bigger disaster – the enormous drain on natural resources diverted from the environment for cultivation and the addition of potentially damaging inputs to sustain the unsustainable.

01

Sprout balls with cashew and fenugreek

It amazes me how small amounts of pulses can produce so much food. I love the combination of humble ingredients to make a satisfying snack or meal, and dishes like this reassure me that healthy eating doesn't need to be expensive or overly complicated. The sprout balls follow a similar process to making falafels, and you can use whatever pulses you like but always keep the chickpeas – that's what holds them together. Soak the pulses overnight to activate enzyme production. These enzymes turn starch into sugar, making nutrients available for the plant or, in our case, for our bodies to digest. I am always looking for ways to increase nutrients in my diet. You can skip the sprouting process (see page 39), but why would you? It's easy and satisfying to watch a pulse transform into a sprout in just a couple of days.

MAKES 35–40 SPROUT BALLS

100 g (3½ oz/⅓ cup) green lentils, sprouted

100 g (3½ oz/¾ cup) chickpeas, sprouted

50 g (1¾ oz/⅓ cup) mung beans, sprouted

50 g (1¾ oz/⅓ cup) Puy lentils, sprouted

½ carrot, roughly chopped

½ red onion, roughly chopped

3 garlic cloves

handful of curly parsley, roughly chopped

½ teaspoon cumin seeds, lightly toasted

½ teaspoon coriander seeds, lightly toasted

1½ teaspoons baking powder

1 teaspoon salt flakes, plus extra to season

1 litre (34 fl oz/4 cups) vegetable oil, for frying

1 × quantity Cashew and fenugreek cream (see page 39), optional

1. Blend the sprouted pulses, carrot, onion, garlic, parsley and toasted spices in a food processor until the mix holds together when squeezed. Tip it into a bowl and stir in the baking powder and salt.

2. Heat the oil to 180°C (360°F). Use two spoons to shape the mixture into oblong-shaped balls about the size of a walnut.

3. Cook the sprout balls in the hot oil, 4–5 at a time. When the sprout balls are evenly coloured and float to the surface they are cooked through, approximately 2 minutes.

4. Remove the sprout balls from the oil, drain on paper towel and season with salt to taste. Repeat with remaining mixture. Serve with the cashew and fenugreek cream.

SPROUTING PULSES

1. Completely cover the pulses (such as lentils, chickpeas and dried beans) in water and soak overnight.

2. The following day, drain and rinse the pulses. Spread the pulses on a tray and cover with a soaking wet tea towel. Pour 200 ml (7 fl oz) of water over the tea towel and leave overnight.

3. The next day, rinse the pulses and the tea towel. Return the pulses to the tray, cover with the wet tea towel, pour over 200 ml water and leave it overnight. Continue this process every day until the pulses begin to sprout.

4. Once the sprouts begins to emerge from the pulses they are ready to use. Sprouted pulses can be stored in a sealed container in the fridge for up to a week.

CASHEW AND FENUGREEK CREAM

*If your aged fenugreek isn't ready, leave it out for now and continue to make the cream following this recipe. It will taste a little different, but still very delicious.

150 g (5½ oz/1 cup) cashew nuts

2 teaspoons Aged fenugreek (see recipe opposite)

zest and juice of 1 lemon (Meyer lemon if possible)

100 ml (3½ fl oz) water

2½ tablespoons grapeseed oil

2½ tablespoons olive oil

1 teaspoon brown rice vinegar

1 garlic clove

salt, to taste

1. Blend all the ingredients in a blender until smooth. Season with salt to taste.

2. Store in an airtight container in the fridge for up to a week.

AGED FENUGREEK

My friend Luke Morgan introduced me to aged fenugreek, and I am forever grateful. Fenugreek seeds are roasted and then covered with apple cider vinegar and left to age for at least three months – the longer you leave it the better it gets. The resulting flavour is interesting to describe – sweet and earthy, yet bright at the same time. The bitterness usually associated with fenugreek disappears, making it a more versatile ingredient. I use the aged fenugreek in curries, relishes, chillies and sauces.

WHAT YOU'LL NEED
- sterilised jar (see page 21)

250 ml (8½ fl oz/1 cup) apple cider vinegar

100 g (3½ oz/½ cup) fenugreek seeds

1. Preheat the oven to 170°C (340°F).

2. Place the fenugreek seeds on a baking tray in a single layer, and roast them in the oven until slightly browned, 12–15 minutes. Let them cool completely on the tray.

3. Place the seeds in a sterilised jar and add enough vinegar to cover the seeds by 3 cm (1¼ in). The seeds will absorb the vinegar over time, so top up with more vinegar to keep them submerged.

4. Age the seeds for at least 3 months (they are best after 12 months).

02

Glazed mushroom skewers

Mushroom skewers were my first and favourite snack at futurefoodsystem. The 'mush-room' (a cabinet designed to grow mushrooms in steam and fresh air funnelled from the bathroom) was key to providing a consistent protein supply, and I was surprised how you could grow mushrooms at home. Humidity and fresh air are essential. Over 12 months we rotated through mushroom varieties, some exotic and many native to Australia. They grew in reusable containers on waste-like spent coffee grounds and sawdust, which we would replace after the mushrooms had flowered two or three times.

Mushrooms are not just delicious. The mycelium below the flowering mushrooms that lives in the top centimetres of the soil plays an integral role in our ecosystem. Mycelium is essential for soil health, carbon absorption and plant communication. When people speak about no-till farming, the aim is to keep this mycelium intact. Science is also revealing a potential link between mushroom consumption and positive brain function. From a culinary perspective, mushrooms are a perfectly sustainable protein, and innovative cultivation processes have made a huge variety available year-round.

In this recipe king oyster and shiitake mushrooms are threaded onto skewers, brushed with a sauce made from mushroom offcuts and grilled on the barbecue. Their texture and depth of flavour could almost be mistaken for those of animal protein.

**MAKES 8 SKEWERS
(IF YOU USE BAMBOO SKEWERS,
SOAK THEM IN WATER FOR
20 MINUTES BEFORE USING)**

3 king oyster mushrooms, sliced in 1½–2 cm (½–¾ in) rounds

16 shiitake or button mushrooms, cut into the same size as the oyster mushrooms

grapeseed oil, for brushing

MUSHROOM GLAZE

150 ml (5 fl oz) Mushroom garum (page 47) or tamari

1 tablespoon miso

1 teaspoon wholegrain mustard

2 tablespoons honey

1 tablespoon brown rice vinegar

1. To make the glaze, combine all the ingredients in a small saucepan and bring it to a gentle simmer over a low heat. Once the honey has completely dissolved, remove the pot from the heat and allow it to cool. The glaze can be stored in an airtight container in the fridge for up to 1 month.

2. Heat a grill to a medium–high heat.

3. Thread the mushrooms onto the skewers, alternating the types of mushrooms, and lightly brush them with the oil.

4. Grill the skewers for 5 minutes on one side, or until the mushrooms begin to caramelise and soften. Turn the skewers and generously brush them with mushroom glaze. Continue to cook until both sides have caramelised, then flip the skewers again and generously brush with more glaze. The mushrooms are done when they are tender and well glazed.

MUSHROOM GARUM

Traditionally, garum is a fermented fish sauce. Fish is fermented with salt and koji (a bacteria grown on rice that's used for fermenting miso and sake). Instead of using fish, this recipe uses mushroom offcuts that are fermented in the same way. This produces an umami-rich sauce that can be used for seasoning or finishing. Garum can be made with other proteins, like meat, by applying the same ratios – equal parts koji rice and protein with the addition of 12 per cent salt to weight. It's a useful way to reduce waste.

WHAT YOU'LL NEED
- 1 × 2-litre jar, sterilised (see page 21)
- seedling raising mat, optional
- cooler box, optional

1 kg (2 lb 3 oz) mushrooms

1 kg (2 lb 3 oz) Koji rice (see recipe opposite)

240 g (8½ oz) fine salt (12%)

1. Chop the mushrooms in a food processor until very finely diced.

2. In a bowl, mix the mushrooms, koji rice and salt until evenly combined.

3. Add the mixture to the sterilised jar, filling the jar three-quarters full. Cut a piece of baking paper into a circle and press onto the surface of the mushroom mix. Seal the jar and keep at 45–58°C (113–136°F) for 3–4 weeks. The easiest way to achieve this is by placing the jars on a seedling raising mat in a closed cooler box.

4. You will need to 'burp' the jar twice in the first week to prevent any 'explosions' or spills. To do this, remove the lid and release the build-up of gas, stir the contents using a sterilised spoon, then refasten the lid.

5. When the garum is ready, the mixture will have separated, with a dark liquid at the base and a 'raft' of rice and mushroom on top. Strain the garum, catching the liquid, and discard the solids. Store the garum in a sterilised jar in the fridge. Garum will get better with age and can keep for years.

KOJI RICE

Koji is a white mould used for fermentation. Like a sourdough starter, it kickstarts fermentation when added to base ingredients like grains or rice. When added to protein, the enzymes present in koji mould convert the protein into amino acids and sugars. These produce flavours that can be described as sweet, savoury, salty and subtly funky. Koji spores can be found in specialty stores and online.

1 kg (2 lb 3 oz) medium-grain rice

10 g (¼ oz) koji spores

1. Soak the rice in plenty of water overnight.

2. The following day, strain the rice, and place it in a medium pot. Rest your index finger vertically on the surface of the rice and add warm water until the water reaches your first knuckle (about 1½ cm/½ in above the rice). Bring the rice to a simmer, stirring occasionally so it doesn't stick. Once simmering, cover, turn heat down to very low and cook for 15 minutes.

3. Soak two tea towels, squeeze out excess water and lay one of the towels flat on a tray. Tip the steaming rice onto the towel.

4. Add the koji spores to a tea strainer or a small sieve. Hold the strainer just above the rice to avoid the spores entering the air and shake a small amount of the spores in a thin, even layer over the mound of rice. Use a fork to mix the rice and spores, and spread it out till it's flat.

5. Sprinkle another layer of spores over the rice, and continue to mix, spread and sprinkle until all of the powder has been used.

6. Spread the rice in an even layer on the tray, cover with the other damp tea towel and keep it at 35–40°C (95–104°F) for two days until a layer of white koji mould appears, making sure the tea towel remains damp throughout. You can keep the tray in your oven with the light on and a bowl of hot water to create some steam to get the right temperature.

7. Once the mould has developed, the koji rice is ready to use, or it can be stored in an airtight container in the fridge for 2–3 weeks or in the freezer for up to 6 months.

03

Cumin wallaby skewers with garlic yoghurt

I've always questioned the culling of native animals, and there are arguments both for and against. In Australia our current mainstream agricultural practices have led to the introduction of government-managed culling programs to control the population of wallabies, whose numbers are thriving because of the availability of food and water. Where the land has been cleared for farming, wallabies get into crops and animal feed, and are seen as pests. There are arguments for the management of macropod populations for their welfare and to minimise environmental degradation. It's a complex and hotly debated issue. I believe that if we cull these animals we should eat them, and we could aim to direct the culling quota into a celebrated kitchen ingredient. Wallabies are free-range, organic and native, have less of an environmental impact than introduced species, as minimum resources are required, and they are delicious. With a subtle flavour and satisfying texture, wallaby meat is also low in fat. These skewers are a simple introduction to cooking wallaby and are a great sustainable alternative to beef or lamb. The spice mix will keep in the pantry for up to 12 months and is a great addition to grilled meat, fish and vegetables.

**MAKES 8 SKEWERS
(IF YOU USE BAMBOO SKEWERS,
SOAK THEM IN WATER FOR
20 MINUTES BEFORE USING)**

500–550 g (1 lb 2 oz–1 lb 3 oz) wallaby loin, sliced into 2 cm (¾ in) strips

1 tablespoon grapeseed oil

½ lemon, to serve

CUMIN SPICE MIX

3 teaspoons cumin seeds

3 teaspoons coriander seeds

¾ teaspoon ground allspice

1 teaspoon salt flakes

GARLIC YOGHURT

200 g (7 oz) natural yoghurt (see recipe opposite)

2 garlic cloves, finely grated

finely grated zest of 1 lemon

1 tablespoon olive oil

salt flakes, to taste

1. For the garlic yoghurt, combine all the ingredients in a small bowl and stir until combined. Set aside until ready to serve.

2. For the spice mix, toast the coriander and cumin seeds in a dry pan over a low heat for 4–5 minutes, or until aromatic. Coarsely crush the seeds in a mortar and pestle. Add the allspice and salt, and stir to combine.

3. Add the wallaby meat, oil and spice mix to a bowl, and toss until the meat is coated. Thread the meat onto the skewers.

4. Place the skewers on a medium–hot grill or barbecue and cook for about 2–3 minutes. Turn the skewers and cook for 2–3 minutes on the other side, or until browned on the outside and medium on the inside. Remove the skewers from the heat and let them rest for a few minutes before serving with the garlic yoghurt and a squeeze of lemon juice.

YOGHURT

When I was 12, I made yoghurt for the first time. Up until then, I thought yoghurt could only be bought from a supermarket, and I thought it was so cool when my aunty whipped up a batch while we were on holidays in beachside Marlo, Victoria. So simple! She heated milk, cooled it and added a spoonful of a previous batch of cultured yoghurt. She covered it and left it on the heater overnight. The next morning the milk had set, and so had my love of milk and the alchemy of dairy products and cheesemaking. This is a recipe for natural yoghurt, but you can add cream, sugar or fruit puree to this recipe and make differently textured or flavoured yoghurts.

WHAT YOU'LL NEED
- cheese measuring spoons, optional
- thermometer
- sterilised pot (see page 21)

---

1 litre (34 fl oz/4 cups) unhomogenised milk

3 tablespoons natural pot set yoghurt (or 1 drop yoghurt starter culture if using a cheese measuring spoon)

---

1. In a clean, sterilised pot, bring the milk to 85°C (185°F) over a medium heat, stirring constantly to prevent it from catching. Remove it from the heat and let it cool to 36°C (97°F). (I do this by plunging the pot directly into a sink filled with ice water). Add the yoghurt or yoghurt culture and allow it to rest for 1 minute, then stir to combine well.

2. Cover the pot and leave it to rest in a warm place (32–38°C/90–100°F) overnight. Do not move the pot while it's resting.

3. The next morning the yogurt will have set. Without disturbing the yoghurt, gently place the pot in the fridge to cool completely before using. It will keep in the fridge for up to 2 weeks.

Cumin wallaby skewers with garlic yoghurt

04

Roasted marrow bones with compound butter on sourdough

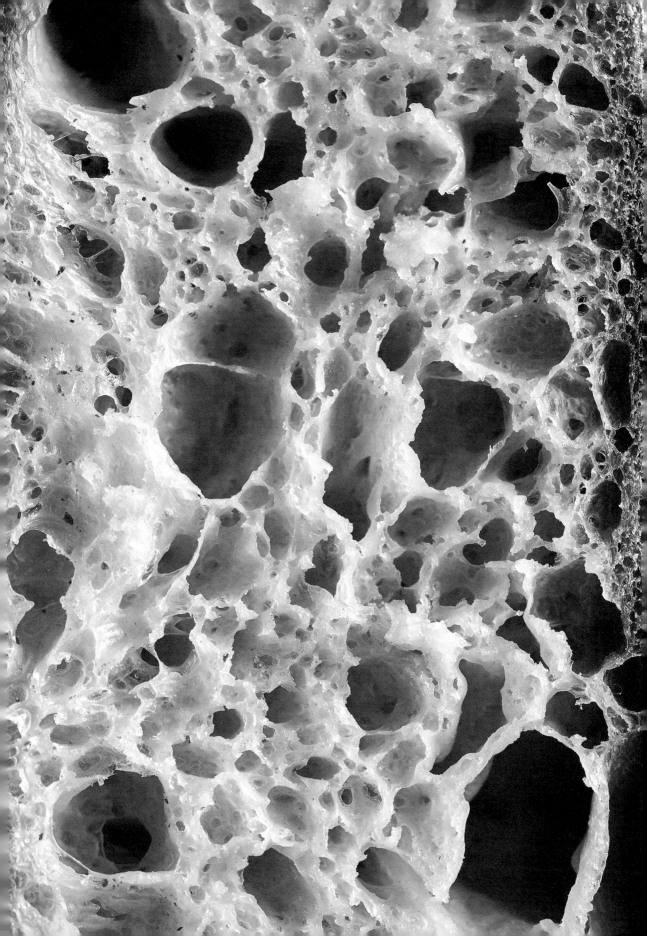

I remember sucking the marrow out of lamb chops as a kid but not enjoying the meat – I've never been an avid meat eater. Cheap, full-flavoured, fatty and packed with nutrients, bone marrow is a great protein. It often gets overlooked and underutilised, but where there's meat, there's bone marrow. As much as this dish screams primal, it's refined, delicate and balanced. This dish works both as a shared starter and as an elegant entrée. Save the roasted bones, as they are ideal for making bone broth.

SERVES 4

100 g (3½ oz) salt (10% salt brine)

1 litre (34 fl oz/4 cups) water

8 × 16 cm (6¼ in) split marrow bones (you can ask your butcher to split them)

4 slices sourdough bread (for a recipe see page 65)

Compound butter, to serve (see recipe opposite)

1. Dissolve the salt in the water to make a brine.

2. Place the bones in a container and pour over the brine, making sure the bones are completely covered. Refrigerate overnight.

3. Preheat the oven to 210°C (410°F) and cover a baking tray with tin foil.

4. Pour off the brine and pat the marrow bones dry using a paper towel.

5. Place the bones cut-side up on the tray, and arrange scrunched up tin foil around and under the bones to make them lie flat.

6. Roast the bones for 15 minutes, or until they start to brown and bubble. Don't overcook them or the marrow will melt away.

7. Meanwhile, toast the sourdough.

8. Remove the marrow bones from the oven and add slices of compound butter on top. Serve with toasted sourdough.

COMPOUND BUTTER METHOD

This flavoured butter is a nice addition to fish, chicken and vegetables.

150 g (5½ oz) butter, at room temperature
1 tablespoon capers, chopped
zest of 1 lemon
1 teaspoon Dijon mustard
1 teaspoon wholegrain mustard
1 shallot, finely diced
1 tablespoon pickled cucumber, finely diced
handful of dill, chopped
handful of flat-leaf (Italian) parsley, chopped
black pepper, to taste

1. Add all the ingredients to a bowl and stir until well combined.

2. Place the butter on a sheet of baking paper, roll it up to form a log and twist the edges to secure.

3. Place the log in the fridge to firm up. The butter will keep for up to 4 weeks in the fridge and up to 3 months in the freezer.

BUTTER

Making butter is easy – simply churn cream until it separates into butter and buttermilk. I've done this a few times unintentionally when whipping cream for desserts! The fat content of the cream determines the amount of butter – the higher the fat content the greater the yield. Fat content is at its highest in winter and spring, when cows eat a varied diet of grass and flowers.

There are two options: a quick method of churning precultured cream, or the lengthier method of culturing the cream yourself before churning. Salt is added to season the butter and prolong its shelf life. It can be added to taste, but a good ratio is 1.5% of the weight of the butter in salt (see page 21). Buttermilk is the by-product of making butter, and it's a useful ingredient for making granita and salad dressings and brining proteins, because of its acidity and tang, so don't let it go to waste.

Quick method

600 ml (12 fl oz) thick (double/heavy) cream
salt

1. Using an electric mixer, whisk the cream on a medium speed until stiff peaks form. Turn the speed down slightly, and continue to whisk until the cream separates completely into butter and buttermilk.

2. Using your hands, remove the butter, squeezing out the buttermilk, and place it in a bowl of ice water. The ice water makes the butter fat solidify and makes it easier to squeeze out all the buttermilk.

3. Squeeze the butter again to remove any remaining buttermilk, and shape it into a ball.

4. Remove the butter from the ice water, and squeeze out any remaining liquid.

5. Weigh the butter and add 1.5% of the weight of the butter in salt (see page 21). Massage the salt into the butter to evenly combine.

6. Place the butter in an airtight container or wrap it in grease-proof paper. The butter will keep for 2–3 weeks in the fridge or up to 3 months in the freezer.

Roasted marrow bones with compound butter on sourdough

CULTURED BUTTER

• cheese measuring spoon
• thermometer

1 litre (34 fl oz/4 cups) thick (double/heavy) cream

½ drop Flora Danica mesophilic aromatic culture
(use a cheese measuring spoon to measure this)

salt

1. In a pot, heat the cream to 85°C (185°F) over a medium heat, stirring continuously to prevent it from sticking.

2. Remove the pot from the heat and immediately place it in a sink or bowl filled with ice water. Stir continuously to prevent a skin forming, and cool the cream to 30°C (86°F).

3. Sprinkle the Flora Danica culture over the surface of the cream and let it sit for 1 minute.

4. Stir the culture into the cream, cover the pot and leave it undisturbed in a draught-free area overnight. The cream will set and thicken.

5. Gently, without agitating the contents, place the pot of cultured cream in the fridge to cool completely.

6. Churn the cultured cream using the Quick method on page 59.

SOURDOUGH BREAD STARTER

People dedicate their whole lives to baking bread;
I dedicated a portion of mine. It was hard, it was
life changing, but I don't regret a moment of it.
Sourdough bread baking is the ultimate skill. You
work with three basic ingredients and a multitude
of variables that you strive to understand and
manage. From the moment the grain is sown to
the time it comes out of the oven, every process
has an impact on your final loaf.

Creating a sourdough culture for bread baking
is a ten-day process of feeding the starter to
develop strength and activity. On day ten it's
ready to be used for bread baking. From this
point on, the ratio of flour and water you feed it
changes, and the starter is referred to as levain.
A drier levain is more forgiving and gives the
sourdough bread a mellow, buttery flavour.

WHAT YOU'LL NEED
- sterilised jar (see page 21)
- thermometer, optional

STARTER/LEVAIN

270 g (9½ oz/1⅔ cups) organic wholemeal
(whole-wheat) flour

Day 1

In a sterilised jar, mix 30 g (1 oz) of the flour and
35 ml (1¼ fl oz) warm water (25–30°C/77–86°F)
to form a paste. Loosely rest the lid on top to
allow for airflow while making sure the starter
doesn't dry out.

Day 2–3

Bubbles may or may not have appeared on the
surface of the paste. Discolouration may also
occur – don't worry, this is natural. Each day,
add 30 g (1 oz) of the flour and 35 ml (1¼ fl oz)
warm water (25–30°C/77–86°F) to the starter
and stir to combine. Cover loosely with the lid.

Day 4–9

Each day, discard 60 g (2 oz) of the starter,
then add 30 g (1 oz) of the flour and 30 ml
(1 fl oz) warm water (25–30°C/77–86°F) to the
remaining starter. Stir until combined and cover
loosely with the lid. The activity in the starter
will build over this time.

Day 10

To keep your starter alive and active you
will need to feed it flour and water each day.
Discarding some of the starter before each
feed allows you to maintain a healthy ratio
of fresh feed to starter. This stops it from
becoming too acidic and inactive. Follow the
levain feed recipe to achieve a continued
successful starter.

LEVAIN FEED

This feed recipe is low in water to produce a stiff
levain and will seem dry to mix at first.

75 g (2¾ oz/½ cup) organic wholemeal
(whole-wheat) flour

2½ tablespoons warm water (25–30°C/77–86°F)

15 g (½ oz) starter

1. Add the flour and water to your jar of starter,
   stir well to combine, and cover loosely with
   a lid. The levain will be ripe (ready to use)
   when bubbles appear evenly throughout,
   approximately 8–12 hours after feeding.

2. To keep the levain alive it must be fed every
   day. On the days you are not making bread,
   discard 90 g (3 oz) of the levain and feed the
   remaining amount. If you know you won't be
   using the levain for a while, you can 'stun' it by
   placing it in the fridge or the freezer. You can
   store it in the fridge for 1 week without feeding
   it. To reactivate the levain, bring it to room
   temperature and feed it for 3 days before
   using it for baking. The levain can be stored
   in the freezer for up to 3 months, but you'll
   need to bring it to room temperature and feed
   it for 2 weeks to reactivate it before using it
   for baking.

Roasted marrow bones with compound butter on sourdough

SOURDOUGH BREAD

When baking sourdough, it's important to fold and stretch the dough during the fermentation process, as it strengthens the dough and allows for even fermentation. This technique brings the cooler dough on the outside into the warmer centre, and creates a more even temperature throughout the process. The dough will become tighter and easier to handle throughout the process, and the appearance of gas bubbles is a sign of activity in the dough.

MAKES 2 LOAVES

440 g (15½ oz/2⅔ cups) baker's flour, plus extra for shaping and dusting

200 g (7 oz/1⅓ cups) organic wholemeal (whole-wheat) flour

530 ml (18 fl oz) warm water (25–30°C/77–86°F)

3 teaspoons (15 g/½ oz) salt

90 g (3 oz) ripe levain (see page 62)

1. In a medium bowl, mix the flours together, add 480 ml (16 fl oz) of the water and stir to combine. Cover with a tea towel and allow the dough to rest for 30 minutes.

2. Add the salt, the remaining water and the ripe levain. Mix the dough by squeezing and folding it over itself. Continue to mix until the water is fully incorporated, the levain is evenly dispersed and the salt has dissolved and can't be felt. The dough may feel slippery and be difficult to mix, but it will come together with continued mixing.

3. Cover the dough and place it in a warm spot for 30 minutes to ferment. Warmth is important to achieve fermentation, so if you are living in a cold environment, you can leave the covered dough in the oven with the light on.

4. Fold the dough by picking up an edge with a slightly wet hand. Lift, stretch and fold the dough to the opposite side of the bowl. Rotating the bowl, work around the edge of the dough twice using this folding technique.

5. Cover the dough and return it to a warm place to ferment for another 30 minutes.

6. Repeat the folding and resting process two more times. After the third fold, rest the dough for 1½–2 hours at 21–24°C (70–75°F).

7. Tip the dough onto a lightly dampened surface and divide it into two even portions. Shape one portion at a time by lifting and folding the outer edge of the dough and pressing it into the centre and holding it so it sticks. Work around the edge of the dough stretching, folding and pressing to form a tight ball.

8. Turn the ball over to expose the tight smooth surface and rest for 15 minutes.

9. Meanwhile, line two medium bowls with tea towels and lightly dust them with flour. Alternatively, you can use bannetons.

10. Lightly sprinkle the surface of each loaf with flour and invert. Use the folding, stretching and pressing technique again to create more tension in the ball and a round loaf. Place the shaped dough, smooth surface down, in the lined bowls or bannetons. If you're baking the bread on the same day, leave the dough to rest for 2–3 hours in a warm spot until it has risen. If you're baking the next day, let the dough rest at room temperature for 1 hour, then move it to the fridge overnight. The next day, remove the dough from the fridge and leave it at room temperature for 1 hour before baking.

11. Preheat the oven to 210°C (410°F). While the oven is heating up, preheat a large tray for the loaves on the middle rack. Fill a second tray with 700 ml (1 lb 9 oz) warm water and place it on the bottom rack to create a steam bath. The steam allows the loaves to expand evenly and assists with browning and crust formation. Alternatively, you can bake the bread in a Dutch oven.

12. Remove the baking tray from the hot oven and place on a heatproof surface. Gently tip the loaves onto the hot tray, leaving 10 cm (4 in) between the loaves to allow for them to expand while baking. Quickly score each loaf by dragging a bread lame (a tool similar to a razor blade) at a slight angle across the surface, about ½ cm (⅛ in) deep. Return the hot tray to the oven immediately, and bake the loaves for 35 minutes.

13. Carefully open the oven door to release the steam. Close the door and bake the bread for a further 8–10 minutes, or until browned. The loaves should sound hollow when tapped. Remove the loaves from the oven and place them on a rack to cool.

Roasted marrow bones with compound butter on sourdough

05

Yabbie
dumplings
with
nasturtium
and chilli oil

Yabbies are freshwater crustaceans. They're native to the eastern and central parts of Australia and found in many inland freshwater dams, rivers and streams. Being scavengers, yabbies don't require specific feed, and are easily farmed and fast growing. If cats have nine lives then yabbies have fifteen. Well, the ones at futurefoodsystem did anyway. With the constant stream of visitors eager to explore an urban food system, it was easy for us to get distracted, but yabbies are a testament to resilience. Our yabbies survived flooded tanks, blocked pipes, predatory trout, curious hands and the occasional escape to the kitchen floor. They actually thrived. We successfully grew yabbies in the aquaponics tanks at futurefoodsystem with trout and freshwater mussels. One of the highlights of our residency was discovering the yabbie babies had hatched, and then watching them mature and go on to reproduce.

Giving the yabbies a quick blanch helps to remove the flesh from the tail and claws but won't cook it all the way through. I prepare most shellfish in a similar way, and this recipe will also work with most types of fish. These dumplings are wrapped in peppery nasturtium leaves, making them gluten free.

SERVES 4

2 kg yabbies (4 lb 6 oz)

1 teaspoon tamari

2 large garlic cloves, crushed

1 teaspoon finely grated ginger

16–20 large nasturtium leaves

chilli oil, to serve

black vinegar, to serve

1. If you are working with live yabbies, place them in the freezer for 30 minutes before cooking to humanely dispatch them.

2. Bring a large pot of water to the boil and prepare a bowl of ice water.

3. Place the yabbies into the boiling water for 40 seconds, then remove them from the pot and immediately submerge them in the ice water to stop the cooking. Remove the flesh from the tails and claws by cracking the shell. Finely chop the meat.

4. Add the yabbie meat, tamari, garlic and ginger to a bowl and mix to combine.

5. Holding a nasturtium leaf in your hand with the stem pointing down between your fingers, place approximately 1 tablespoon of the mixture on the centre and fold the leaf around the filling to enclose it. Refrigerate until ready to cook.

6. Preheat a steam oven to 100°C (212°F) and line a tray with baking paper. Alternatively, place a bamboo steamer lined with baking paper over a pot of boiling water.

7. Place the dumplings, fold down, on the tray or steamer with the stem facing up and steam for 2–3 minutes, or until firm when pressed. Serve with chilli oil and a drizzle of black vinegar.

CHILLI OIL

I always have a jar of chilli oil on the go for adding to stir-fries, rice, steamed vegetables and fish dishes. It brings life to simple ingredients by enhancing the flavour. I also take it on the road when cooking outdoors. Try different flavour combinations like curry oil, herb oil or mushroom oil.

WHAT YOU'LL NEED
• sterilised jars (see page 21)

2 tablespoons fennel seeds

3½ tablespoons coriander seeds

1 tablespoon cumin seeds

1 tablespoon Sichuan peppercorns

1½ teaspoons whole black peppercorns

3½ tablespoons sesame seeds

4 cardamom pods

2–3 star anise

40 g (1½ oz) chilli flakes

1½ teaspoon ground allspice

40 garlic cloves (approx. 250 g/9 oz), thinly sliced

900 ml (30½ fl oz) grapeseed oil

5 shallots, thinly sliced

1½ tablespoons salt flakes

3 tablespoons tamari

2 tablespoons brown rice vinegar

1. In a dry pan, toast the fennel seeds, coriander seeds, cumin seeds, peppercorns and sesame seeds until aromatic.

2. Using a mortar and pestle, lightly crush the toasted spices to break them. Transfer the spice mix to a large heatproof bowl. Add the cardamon, star anise, chilli flakes and allspice to the bowl.

3. Add the garlic and 400 ml (13½ fl oz) of the oil to a small pot. In another pot, add the shallots and the remaining 500 ml (17 fl oz/2 cups) of oil. Place the pots over a medium heat and cook, stirring, for about 15 minutes, or until the garlic and shallots begin to fry and turn golden brown.

4. Place a heatproof sieve over the bowl of spices. Pour in the hot oil from both pots, stir and leave it to cool. Remove the garlic and shallot from the sieve, and place them on paper towel to cool.

5. Once cool and crisp, lightly crush the fried garlic and shallots between your fingers, and add them to the oil. Add the salt, tamari and vinegar and stir to combine.

6. Pour the oil into sterilised jars and store them at room temperature. Once open, keep in the fridge for 12 months or longer.

06

Barramundi and sorghum tostadas with pickled jalapeños and green coriander seeds

To eat fish or not to eat fish. That is a question for our time, as the biomass of our oceans is rapidly depleting. Currently, I only eat seafood that I've caught myself or has been caught by someone I know, as I think it's the ethical thing to do. Like many, I worry about the future of our oceans, and I'm happy to go without seafood if it means populations of fish and corals have a fighting chance to recover. Overfishing and community awareness of fish provenance has made way for a new age of farmed fish; not soft and mushy, but sustainably grown and delicious. Barramundi, trout, Murray cod and cobia are on my menu, but we still need to be aware of what farmed fish are being fed and how and where they are farmed.

SERVES 4

400 g (14 oz) barramundi fillets, skin removed

1 teaspoon fine salt

zest of 1 lime and juice of ½ lime

4 tablespoons (80 g/¾ oz) Aioli (see page 135)

3 tablespoons vegetable oil

1 × quantity Sorghum tostadas (see page 80)

Pickled jalapeños (see recipe opposite), to serve

Green coriander seeds (see recipe opposite), to serve

½ bunch coriander (cilantro), to serve

1. Sprinkle the fish evenly with the salt. The salt seasons the fish and makes the flesh slightly firmer. Place the fish on a tray and let it rest in the fridge for 30 minutes.

2. Meanwhile, add the lime zest and juice to the aioli and stir to combine.

3. Pat the barramundi dry with a piece of paper towel, and heat the oil in a frying pan over a medium–high heat.

4. Cook the fish for 4–5 minutes, or until it begins to turn golden brown. When the surface of the flesh feels just warm to touch, turn the fish and cook for a further 30–60 seconds, then remove it from the heat.

5. Spread a layer of lime aioli onto the tostadas and, using your hands or tongs, add flakes of fish on top. Top with jalapeños, coriander seeds and coriander. Serve.

GREEN CORIANDER SEEDS

This recipe revolutionised my green-seed game. Green coriander seeds are explosions of bright floral freshness that are hard to describe – you just need to try them. When a coriander plant comes to the end of its life, its energy moves to producing seeds for reproduction. The leaves shrink and flowers bloom. Growers often remove their plants at this stage; however, the seeds are the best bit. It's common to find dried seeds in the pantry, but preserved green seeds can elevate a sweet or savoury dish to another level. Preserve them in a 1:1 sugar syrup for sweet applications, or cover them with salt, like you would capers, and add them to salsas, salads, stir-fries and dressings.

WHAT YOU'LL NEED
• sterilised jar (see page 21)

green coriander seeds

fine salt

1. Place the seeds into a sterilised jar and add enough salt to coat. You want enough salt to cover any gaps between the seeds but not so much you can't see the colour and outline of the seeds through the jar.

2. You can use the seeds straight away, but they will keep in the fridge for 4–6 months. Over time, the seeds will begin to change colour slightly, but the bright flavour will remain.

PICKLED JALAPEÑOS

Sweet pickles are great for moderating heat and enhancing flavour. If you don't want to cook the ingredient you're pickling, cool the pickling liquid before adding it to retain the colour and texture of your pickles.

WHAT YOU'LL NEED
• 2 sterilised jars (see page 21)

250 g (9 oz) jalapeños, thinly sliced

350 ml (12 fl oz) white wine vinegar

3 teaspoons salt

3½ tablespoons (45 g/1½ oz) caster (superfine) sugar

1. Put the chilli slices in the sterilised jars.

2. Heat the vinegar, salt, sugar and 400 ml (13½ fl oz) of water in a small pot over a medium heat, and cook until the sugar and salt have dissolved. Remove the pot from the heat and let the liquid cool completely.

3. Pour the pickling liquid over the chilli, making sure it's completely covered. Seal the jars and store in the fridge for up to 12 months.

Barramundi and sorghum tostadas with pickled jalapeños and green coriander seeds

SORGHUM TOSTADAS

Nixtamalisation is typically the process of cooking maize in an alkaline solution. Maize has an outer layer that is removed during the nixtamalisation process, and the alkaline solution can be made by adding calcium hydroxide to water. Removing the outer layer makes the nutrients easier to digest and absorb, and it also means you can turn the kernels into a dough (called masa), which can be steamed, grilled or fried for items like tacos, tortillas and tostadas. Sorghum is a small grain native to Africa and Australia. It is a nitrogen fixing, efficient crop that does well in dry conditions, and it has a similar structure to corn and maize. Because of the similarities, I like to nixtamalise sorghum, too, and the result is delicious. It takes two days to do, and the masa can be stored in the fridge for up to ten days.

WHAT YOU'LL NEED

• two silicone mats, optional

250 g (9 oz/1 cup plus 1 tablespoon) sorghum

1 teaspoon calcium hydroxide, dissolved in 1 tablespoon water

generous pinch of salt flakes

1 litre (34 fl oz/4 cups) vegetable oil, plus extra for greasing

1. Add the sorghum, calcium hydroxide solution and 750 ml (25½ fl oz/3 cups) of water to a medium pot and bring it to a simmer over a medium heat. Cook for 25–30 minutes, or until the sorghum is just tender (take a grain and squeeze it between your fingers – when it flattens it's ready). Remove the pot from the heat, cover with a lid and leave to rest at room temperature overnight.

2. Drain the sorghum and rinse it with cold running water to wash away the husk and expose the grain. You will need to stir the grain with your hands to wash it all away. Drain away as much water as you can so the grain isn't wet.

3. Add the sorghum and salt to a food processor, and blend to form a dough. Scrape down the sides occasionally for an even texture.

4. In a medium pot, heat the oil to 180°C (360°F) over a medium heat.

5. Lightly oil your hands and two silicone mats or pieces of baking paper. Place the dough between the mats or paper and roll out the dough till it's about 1–1½ mm (³⁄₆₄–¹⁄₁₆ in) thick. Use a knife to cut the sheet into triangles (approximately 8–10 cm wide), then gently peel them off the mat.

6. Carefully add 3–4 triangles to the hot oil, and cook for 2–3 minutes, or until lightly puffed. Remove the triangles from the oil using a slotted spoon, and drain on a plate lined with paper towel to get them crisp. Repeat with the remaining dough. Sprinkle the tostadas with a small amount of salt. These are best eaten on the same day, but, once completely cool, they can be stored in an airtight container in the pantry for up to 4 days.

07

Stuffed potato cakes with tomato-chilli relish

These potato cakes also work well stuffed with leftovers, such as vegetables, smoked fish, fresh curds or bolognese. They can be quick snacks, a key dinner served with a salad or even eaten for breakfast. The potato flour and egg yolk are what holds the potato cakes together and make them easy to fry.

MAKES 14 POTATO CAKES

4 potatoes (about 850–900 g/ 1 lb 14 oz–2 lb), cut into 3 cm (1¼ in) cubes

1 egg yolk

50 g (1¾ oz/4 tablespoons plus 1 teaspoon) potato flour, plus extra for dusting

1 tablespoon olive oil, plus extra for frying

salt and pepper, to season

FILLING

3 tablespoons olive oil

1 onion, finely diced

3 garlic cloves, sliced

1 bunch silverbeet, leaves and stems roughly sliced

3 spring onions (scallions), green and white parts, sliced

100 ml (3½ fl oz) white wine, optional

1 handful dill, roughly chopped

1 handful flat-leaf (Italian) parsley, roughly chopped

1 teaspoon ground allspice

pinch of nutmeg

salt and pepper, to season

zest of ½ lemon

1. For the filling, heat the oil in a medium pot over a medium heat. Cook the onion and garlic until tender, about 10 minutes. Add the silverbeet and spring onion and stir to coat with the oil. Deglaze the pot with the white wine, if using.

2. Turn the heat down to low, and cook the greens for 20 minutes, or until tender. Add the herbs and spices, season with salt and pepper, and cook for a further 5–10 minutes. Add the lemon zest, transfer to a bowl and let the mixture cool.

3. For the potato cakes, place the potatoes into a pot with 2 cm (¾ in) of water, bring it to a simmer, and cook for 15 minutes, or until tender.

4. Drain the potatoes then push them through a potato ricer, or mash them using a potato masher or a fork. Allow them to cool slightly then add the egg yolk, potato flour, oil, salt and pepper. Mix to form a smooth 'dough'.

5. Line a tray with baking paper. Using your hands, take 3 tablespoons of the potato dough and press it to form a disc. Place 1 tablespoon of the filling in the centre of the disc, fold the potato dough over the filling and press it into a puck shape. Repeat with remaining dough and filling.

6. Heat oil in a frying pan over a medium heat. Cook the potato cakes for 6–8 minutes, turning once, until golden on both sides. Serving with tomato–chilli relish (page 89).

TOMATO-CHILLI RELISH

A good relish is determined by its versatility, even when it has distinct punchy flavours. The balance between sweetness, acidity and saltiness in this relish allows it to accompany most dishes, and those three elements also help to preserve it. No matter what ingredients you choose for your relish, specific visual cues will tell you when it's ready for bottling – you're aiming for a glossy, jammy texture. If it's too loose, the relish will be soggy and have a short shelf life.

MAKES 2 LITRES (68 FL OZ/8 CUPS)

WHAT YOU'LL NEED
• sterilised jars (see page 21)

3 tablespoons olive oil

3 red onions, diced

5 garlic cloves, sliced

1 tablespoon cumin seeds

4 teaspoons smoked paprika

100 g (3½ oz/1 cup) chilli flakes

300 g (10½ oz) tomato paste (concentrated puree)

1½ kg (3 lb 5 oz) tomatoes, roughly diced

150 ml (5 fl oz) sherry vinegar

100 g (3½ oz/½ cup lightly packed) brown sugar

150 g (5½ oz/⅔ cup) caster (superfine) sugar

5 teaspoons salt

1. Heat the oil in a medium pot over a low heat. Add the onion and garlic and cook for 20 minutes, or until tender.

2. Add the cumin, paprika and chilli, and cook for 2–3 minutes. Add the tomato paste, and cook, stirring continuously, until it begins to bubble, then add the tomatoes. Cook, stirring occasionally, for 45–50 minutes, or until the mixture has reduced by three-quarters.

3. Add the vinegar, sugars and salt, and cook for a further 15–20 minutes, or until thick and glossy.

4. When the relish begins to thicken and becomes glossy, test it by dragging a spoon down the centre – it's ready when it slowly joins back together. Immediately spoon the hot mix into sterilised jars, tightly close the jars and let them cool to room temperature. The relish will keep 12 months and should be stored in the fridge once opened.

08

Freshly milled flatbread with 'nduja and sweet onion

This recipe produces a sophisticated and satisfying result and is an introduction to bread and charcuterie making at an elementary level. I use the same dough recipe for barbecue flatbreads and pizza bases, but I use less water for a pizza dough. Wholegrains that are freshly milled retain more flavour and nutrients. Freshly milled flour is active and alive, which is great for your gut.

SERVES 8–10

FLATBREAD

2 teaspoons (7 g/¼ oz) dried yeast

450 g (1 lb) plain (all-purpose) or baker's flour

150 g (5½ oz) freshly milled flour (see page 97)

2 tablespoons olive oil, plus extra for greasing

2 teaspoons salt

375 g (13 oz) 'Nduja (see page 97)

150 g (5½ oz) Sweet onion (see below)

basil leaves, to serve

SWEET ONION

3 brown onions, sliced

2 tablespoons olive oil

2 teaspoons salt

1. Mix the yeast and both flours in a medium bowl. In another bowl, combine the oil with 480 ml (16 fl oz) of water.

2. Add 330 ml (11 fl oz) of the water and oil mixture to the flours, and use your hands to mix it together to form a rough dough, making sure everything is well combined.

3. Mix in the salt and the remaining 150 ml (5 fl oz) of liquid. The dough will become sticky. Knead the dough until it's smooth, then place it in a large oiled bowl, cover it with a tea towel and let it rest for 45 minutes.

4. Once rested, stretch and fold the dough over itself to knock back the gas bubbles and build strength, then let it rest for 1 hour.

5. Grease a 20 × 30 cm (8 × 12 in) baking tin. Add the dough and let it rest for a further 40 minutes, or until gas bubbles appear on the surface.

6. Meanwhile, make the sweet onion. Heat the olive oil in a small frying pan over a medium–low heat. Add the sliced onions and cook for 15–20 minutes, or until they become translucent and tender. Season with salt. Remove the onion from the pan and set aside in the fridge till needed. It can be prepared ahead of time and will keep in the fridge for up to 2 weeks.

7. Preheat the oven to 190°C (375°F).

8. Once the dough has rested, top it with the sweet onion and use your finger tips to press it into the dough. Bake for 25–30 minutes.

9. When the bread begins to colour, top it with torn pieces of 'nduja and continue baking for 8–10 minutes. The bread is ready when it has a golden colour and the 'nduja begins to crisp. Top the flatbread with basil leaves and serve.

'NDUJA

'Nduja is a highly spiced spreadable sausage. It can be cured in the fridge and is one of the easiest cured meats to make, so it's a good introduction to curing meats. Watch salt work its magic over time, changing the texture and highlighting the subtle flavours of the meat. This recipe requires a mincer, but the mix gets wrapped in muslin cloth, so you don't need a sausage stuffer. It's important to work cleanly when making charcuterie, and the ingredients and equipment must be cold to prevent spoilage and ensure a longer shelf life. Sterilise the benches, equipment and your hands before you start, to make the process simple and worry free.

MAKES 2 SAUSAGES

WHAT YOU'LL NEED
- mincer
- two 50 × 50 cm (19¾ × 19¾ in) pieces of muslin
- butcher's twine
- gloves

500 g (1 lb 2 oz) pork backfat
250 g (9 oz) pork belly
1½ teaspoons fennel seeds
1½ teaspoons whole black peppercorns
⅓ cup chili flakes
250 g (9 oz) long red chilli, seeded (keep the seeds in for a spicy 'nduja)
1 tablespoon fine salt
2½ tablespoons smoked paprika

1. Dice the pork fat and the pork belly into small pieces that will fit into the mincer. Place the pork fat in the freezer while you prepare the other ingredients.

2. Toast the fennel seeds in a dry pan over a medium heat for 1–2 minutes, or until fragrant. Roughly crush the fennel seeds, peppercorns and chilli flakes using a mortar and pestle. Finely chop the chillies in a food processor.

3. Using a mincer on the coarse setting, mince the chilled pork fat then the pork belly into a large bowl.

4. Add the fennel seed mix, chilli, salt and paprika and use gloved hands to mix until evenly combined.

5. Lay out the muslin. Divide the mixture into two even portions, and slap each portion back and forth between your hands to remove any air pockets and form a ball. Place each ball on a piece of muslin. Bring all four corners together and twist to wrap and tightly squeeze the 'nduja. Secure with the butcher's twine.

6. Hang the bundles in the fridge for two weeks to cure – they will feel firm when ready. Alternatively, you can place them on wire racks; the important thing is to create airflow around the bundles. The 'nduja will keep 3–4 weeks in the fridge.

MILLING GRAINS

There are a few simple ways to mill grain: stone grinding and steel cutting. Grinding grains between stones to make flour is an ancient method, and stone milling is the traditional process of pressing grains through two round stones to produce flour. The mechanism is a bit like that of a big pepper grinder. If you see a product labelled 'stoneground flour', this is the process it's been through. Another method of milling grain is by steel cutting, where the grain is cut instead of ground – imagine a blender. Most people don't have a flour mill at home, so in this recipe I use a blender, such as a Thermomix or Nutribullet.

whole grains

1. Place the grains into the blender and blend on high until the grain turns into a fine powder. This will take approximately 1 minute depending on your blender. Be cautious of the temperature of the flour, as it will heat because of the friction. If it begins to feel warm to the touch, stop blending and allow the grain to cool before continuing, as heat can denature the enzymes in the flour.

09

Zucchini and fermented bean rice cakes

Basic fermenting is an essential skill if you want to capitalise on seasonal abundance for use later in the year. Green beans were the first ingredient I picked to ferment at futurefoodsystem. We hadn't finished building the kitchen, so I fermented all 6 kg of them. When we opened for dinner almost three months later, guess what?! Fired fermented beans went on the menu. The thing I like best about fermenting is using the fermented ingredient in dishes. It adds depth with lactic tang and acidity with little effort. That's exactly what it does for these rice cakes.

SERVES 4

1 zucchini, very thinly sliced lengthways

12 Fermented beans (see page 105), or pickled beans, very roughly chopped

4 spring onions (scallions), green and white parts, sliced

1 long green chilli, sliced

handful of basil leaves, torn

2 tablespoons oil

Tomato–chili relish (see page 89), to serve

BATTER

50 g (1¾ oz/1½ cups) besan (chickpea flour)

50 g (1¾ oz/⅓ cup) brown rice flour

1 teaspoon baking powder

pinch of salt flakes

1. For the batter, mix all the ingredients with 130 ml (4½ fl oz) of water and stir to combine.

2. Add the zucchini, beans, spring onion, chilli and basil to the bowl and fold them through the batter to combine, making sure everything is well coated.

3. Heat the oil in a frying pan over a medium heat. Use your fingers to pinch portions of coated vegetables and gently squeeze them together as you place them into the hot oil. Cook for 2–3 minutes, or until golden brown, then turn and cook for a further 2 minutes until cooked through. Serve with tomato-chilli relish.

FERMENTED BEANS

Fermentation is one of the oldest and simplest forms of food preservation. Lacto-fermentation is a natural anaerobic process where microorganisms break down starch and convert it into lactic acid, which gives lacto-fermented foods a unique acidic tang and provides numerous health benefits, such as adding probiotics to your diet, contributing to a healthy microbiome and aiding digestion. Salt is added to control the anaerobic environment to prevent the growth of harmful bacteria and preserve the ingredient.

WHAT YOU'LL NEED
• sterilised jars (see page 21)

green beans

2% salt brine (2% salt to water, see page 21)

1. To make the brine, mix salt and water until the salt has dissolved. Place the whole beans in the sterilised jars and pour over the salt brine, leaving 3-4 cm (1¼ -1½ in) of space between the brine and the top of the jars. Close the jars and leave them out on the bench.

2. For the next 5–7 days, open the jars daily to 'burp' the ferment and release any gasses that begin to develop. Once the beans taste funky and acidic, place the jars into the fridge to slow down the fermentation. The beans will keep for 3 months.

Zucchini and fermented bean rice cakes

10

Garden
bread

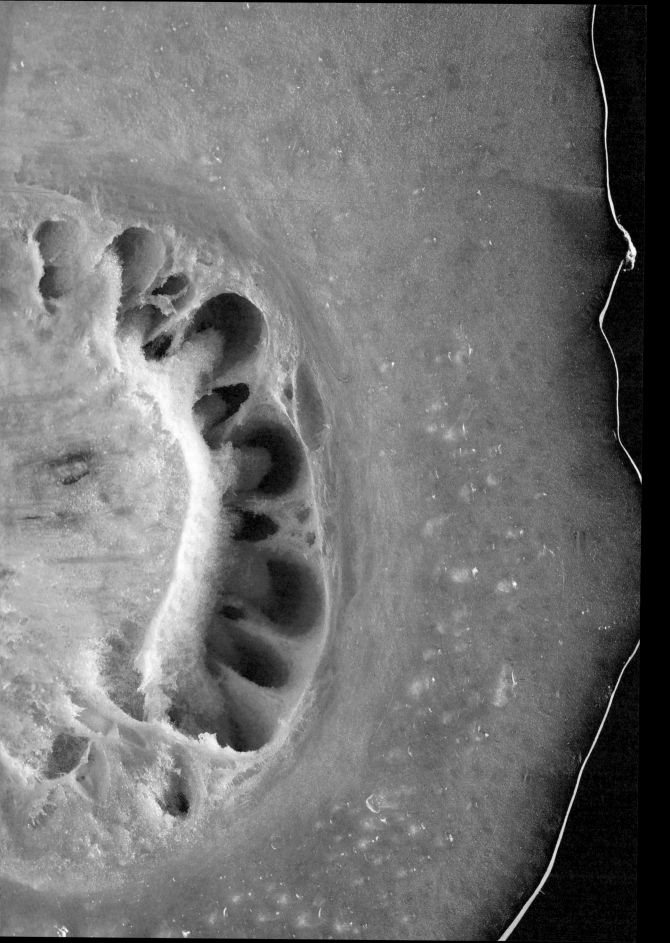

Garden bread is a gluten- and dairy-free quick bread. The texture is similar to that of cornbread but achieved without using animal fat or buttermilk. Instead, pumpkin puree and grapeseed oil bind the batter and eliminate the need for gums and emulsifiers that are often found in store-bought gluten-free baked goods. You can switch out pumpkin for any vegetable puree that has a similar texture. Leek is another favourite. Top the bread with any veg, seeds, herbs or spices that you like.

MAKES 1 BREAD

200 g (7 oz) Pumpkin puree, cold (see recipe opposite)

1 egg

180 ml (6 fl oz) grapeseed oil

150 g (5½ oz/¾ cup) maize

150 g (5½ oz/¾ cup) polenta

1½ teaspoons baking powder

¼ teaspoon garlic powder

1 teaspoon salt flakes

olive oil, for drizzling

TOPPINGS

red onion, thinly sliced

zucchini, shaved

tomatoes, sliced

basil leaves

chilli flakes

1. Preheat oven to 180°C (360°F) and line a 20 × 20 cm (8 × 8 in) baking tin with baking paper.

2. Combine the pumpkin puree, egg, oil and 230 ml (8 fl oz) of water in a bowl. In a separate large bowl combine the maize, polenta, baking powder, garlic powder and salt.

3. Add the wet mix to the dry mix and stir till well combined. Pour the batter into the lined tin and top with an even layer of shaved vegetables, herbs and seasonings of choice.

4. Drizzle with a small amount of oil then place the tin into the oven for 25–30 minutes, or until cooked through. When the bread is done, a skewer inserted will come out clean. Remove from the oven and cool slightly before serving.

PUMPKIN PUREE

500 g (1 lb 2 oz) pumpkin (winter squash), thinly sliced

1. Place the pumpkin in a pot and add 1 cm (½ in) of water. Cover the pot and steam the pumpkin over a medium heat for 15 minutes, or until tender.

2. Drain the pumpkin and puree it in a food processor until smooth. Cool completely before using in the Garden bread, or store in the freezer for up to 3 months and defrost when required.

11

Avocado salsa with parsley-seed dressing and eggs on toast

It wouldn't be my book without a recipe featuring fried eggs and avocado. I grew up in Melbourne, the avo toast capital of the world, and eggs are my everything, but this recipe is really all about the dressing. I don't need to tell anyone how to fry an egg, but you need to make this dressing and drizzle it on all your favourite ingredients. The dressed avocado goes well as an alternative salsa with tacos and can be used as a dip similar to guacamole.

SERVES 2

2 avocados, diced

1 small shallot, finely diced

salt flakes, to taste

juice of ½ lemon

large knob of butter, plus extra for spreading

4 eggs

4 slices of sourdough

generous handful of watercress, for garnish

PARSLEY SEED DRESSING

1½ tablespoons Herb flower and seed oil (see recipe opposite)

2 teaspoons brown rice vinegar

1. To make the dressing, combine the ingredients in a small bowl.

2. Combine the avocado, shallot, salt, lemon juice and parsley seed dressing in a bowl and gently toss to combine. Try not to squish the avocado.

3. Melt the butter in a medium frying pan over a medium heat, and fry the eggs to your liking. Toast and butter the bread.

4. Top the toast with the avocado and a fried egg and garnish with watercress.

HERB FLOWER AND SEED OIL

Herb seeds and flowers are underutilised ingredients. If I see a plant going to seed on the street, I will always pinch a handful of these tiny flavour bombs. Don't be fooled by the simplicity of this oil. You can thank me later.

WHAT YOU'LL NEED
• sterilised jar (see page 21)

fresh parsley seeds and flowers (or other herbs, such as fennel, sage, basil, coriander (cilantro), dill or thyme

salt

olive oil

1. Add generous pinches of salt flakes to a mortar, lay the herb seeds and flowers on top, then crush the herbs into the salt.

2. Drizzle enough oil over the seeds to completely submerge them, then stir to combine and evenly disperse the herbs and seeds. Pour the oil into a sterilised jar. The oil will last for months in a cool, dry place and will take on more flavour over time.

Avocado salsa with parsley-seed dressing and eggs on toast

117

12

Broccoli, buckwheat and seaweed salad

Seaweed is the food of our future. It's high in vitamins and minerals, fast growing (some say 30 times faster than land plants!) and abundant. Could algae be one of the most important life forms on this planet along with fungi? I think so! Farmed seaweed is being used in animal feeds to reduce the amount of methane being produced by cattle, and in fish feed to reduce the capture of wild-caught fish. The rehydrated wakame seaweed flakes used in this recipe complement this salad's crisp, crunchy and creamy textures.

SERVES 4

2 tablespoons dried wakame flakes

1 large head of broccoli (about 400 g/14 oz), finely shaved

50 g (1¾ oz/¼ cup) buckwheat

3 tablespoons Diced dressing (see page 125)

1 × quantity Macadamia milk (see page 125)

1. Hydrate the wakame in 200 ml (7 fl oz) of cold water for 1–2 minutes. Once plump and tender, strain and set aside. Toast the buckwheat in a pan over a medium heat until golden. Set aside to cool.

2. Add the broccoli, buckwheat, hydrated wakame and dressing to a bowl and toss to evenly combine.

3. Pour the macadamia milk into the base of a serving bowl and top with the dressed broccoli salad. Serve.

MACADAMIA MILK

Raw macadamia milk is the queen of nut milks and an easy way to add a silky and fatty mouth feel to a vegetarian or vegan dish. The flavour is subtle when the nuts are raw, and this is how I prefer to make the milk, but if you want a nuttier flavour, you can roast the macadamias until lightly golden brown in a low–moderate oven before moving onto the blending process.

75 g (2¾ oz/½ cup) macadamia nuts

3 teaspoons grapeseed oil

½ teaspoon tamari

1 teaspoon sherry vinegar

salt, to taste

1. In a food processor, blend the macadamias, oil and 100 ml (3½ fl oz) of cold water into a smooth puree. Season with the tamari, sherry vinegar and salt. The macadamia milk will keep in the fridge for 1 week.

DICED DRESSING

Diced dressing is the 'little black dress' of dressings. Use it to finish soups or garnish roast vegetables, add it to BBQ meals or pasta, or serve it with poultry and fish. Handy to have in the fridge, it lasts for weeks. The ratios in this recipe work well with different combinations of herbs and spices.

WHAT YOU'LL NEED
• sterilised jar (see page 21)

pinch of saffron

2½ tablespoons chardonnay vinegar

1 teaspoon coriander seeds

1 teaspoon fennel seeds

4 shallots, very finely diced

4 long red chillies, deseeded and finely chopped

3 long green chillies, deseeded and finely chopped

4 thyme sprigs, leaves picked and roughly chopped

1 tablespoon finely chopped coriander (cilantro) stems

180 ml (6 fl oz) olive oil

salt and pepper, to taste

1. Add the saffron and vinegar to a small bowl, and stir to hydrate the saffron and transfer the flavour and colour. Set aside.

2. Toast the fennel and coriander seeds in a dry frying pan over a medium heat, then lightly crush using a mortar and pestle.

3. Add the crushed seeds, shallot, chillies, thyme, coriander stem and oil to the saffron vinegar and season with salt and pepper to taste. The dressing will keep in a sterilised jar in the fridge for up to 1 month.

Broccoli, buckwheat and seaweed salad

13

Smoked trout with celeriac and spring onion remoulade

Take a share house of idealistic twenty-somethings, one industrial grade plastic container split in two and a dozen rainbow trout – my first foray into aquaponics was a recipe for disaster. The theory is simple enough: the fish live below in the watery half and the water is pumped up onto a bed of edible plants above. Fish waste is then filtered out to feed the plants and the clean water is recycled back into the fish tank. Happy fish, happy plants, right? Sadly, no. There were deaths, and nearly 10 years on, it still haunts me. We were hugely enthusiastic but, unfortunately, we assumed too much.

Fish need a consistent supply of oxygenated water to survive and thrive and our system fell short on the technical requirements. Panic and regret. That's what I felt when confronted with some of our more obvious oversights. I felt responsible, so when Joost insisted on aquaponics systems at futurefoodsystem, I shuddered.

More than any other system in the house, our two aquaponics set-ups demanded most of our time and attention. One single tank housed barramundi and a second system with three tanks was home to rainbow trout, fresh water mussels and yabbies. Already hyper vigilant from my previous nightmare, now I can only laugh at the obstacles we encountered and the lengths we went to to keep those creatures alive.

Building a three-story, off-grid, sustainable house that grows all its own food for its occupants in the middle of Melbourne's CBD as a social experiment and 'pop-up' had complexities we couldn't possibly predict, and nearly all of them impacted the fish. Inconsistent power from our solar panels and battery wall, tradespeople unplugging power points for tools, a power-off button visitors thought was a doorbell, Melbourne's varying weather (hot one day, freezing the next), the balance of harvesting and replanting, the size of the trout compared to the size of the pipes and floating carrots all leading to new unintentional internal water features. Then there was making fish food and testing the water, and I can tell you, when it comes time to harvest the fish, 'like shooting fish in a barrel' does not apply. There was also the time a trout flung itself from the tank and fell three stories past a wide-eyed Zac Efron.

I've learnt a lot and growing trout can be 100 per cent simpler than our experience. I've spent enough time with trout to know I love them – they're a fast-growing fish that can be farmed safely and sustainably, that's easy to cook and, most of all, that's delicious.

SERVES 4

150 g (5½ oz/½ cup) Aioli (see page 135)

1 tablespoon capers, chopped

small handful of chopped dill

4 spring onions (scallions), finely sliced

zest and juice of ½ lemon

1 celeriac (about 400 g/14 oz), peeled and cut into 5 × 5 mm (¼ × ¼ in) batons

salt, to taste

1 × Smoked trout, skin and bones removed, flaked (see page 132)

1. Add the aioli, capers, dill, spring onions and lemon zest and juice to a bowl and stir to combine.

2. Fold the aioli mix into the celeriac and season with salt to taste, then gently fold through the flaked trout. Serve.

SMOKED TROUT

Smoking is another traditional method of food preservation. Growing up, I was never a fan of cold cuts or anything smoked; they were always dry and way too smoky. My perception changed at Oakridge when smoking trout became my favourite prep job. Now it's an ingredient I love to cook with. Curing the fish before smoking imparts flavour and helps it retain colour and moisture. You can also use this technique with other proteins and vegetables, adjusting the cooking times and temperatures according to what you're cooking.

WHAT YOU'LL NEED
- smoker or charcoal grill with a lid
- smoking chips or bay leaf branches, soaked in cold water
- digital thermometer

1 × 400–500 g (14½ oz–1 lb 2 oz) rainbow trout, cleaned and scaled

SALT CURE

20 g (1 tablespoon) fine salt

20 g (¾ oz/4 teaspoons) caster (superfine) sugar

½ teaspoon coriander seeds

½ teaspoon whole black peppercorns

1 bay leaf (preferably fresh)

zest of 1 mandarin

1. For the salt cure, stir all the ingredients together in a small bowl.

2. Sprinkle the salt cure over the trout and inside the gut cavity. Place the salted fish on a rack and in a container or on a tray to catch any drips, and place it in the fridge to cure overnight.

3. The following day, rinse off the salt cure under cold running water and pat the fish dry with paper towels.

4. Place the fish on a rack or tray, uncovered, and put it back in the fridge for at least 4 hours or overnight. This allows the skin to become tacky and allows the smoke to adhere to the fish – the skin coating is called pellicle.

5. Smoke the fish using one of the following methods.

How to hot smoke with a smoker

There are two types of smoking – hot smoking and cold smoking. As the name implies, cold smoking takes place in a smoky environment that imparts flavour without applying any heat that may influence the texture of the item being smoked. Smoked cheeses are an example of cold smoked foods. They take on flavour without any heat, as any temperature increase would melt the cheese. Hot smoking imparts flavour and temperature, which impacts the texture of the ingredient being smoked. The food is gently cooked and the smoke is imparted throughout the cooking process.

1. Preheat the smoker to 110°C (230°F), then add the smoking chips or bay leaf branches to create smoke.

2. Hot smoke the trout to an internal temperature of 58°C (154°F) on a digital thermometer. Insert the probe into the thickest part of the fillet. Remove the fish from the smoker and allow it to cool and set slightly before using. Alternatively store in the fridge for 1–1½ weeks.

How to hot smoke without a smoker

1. Light a coal grill and let it burn down to glowing coals. We are looking to create an environment between 130–140°C (266–285°F) when the lid is on. Place the smoking chips or bay branches on the hot coals.

2. Place the fish on the grill rack and cover with the lid to trap the smoke. Leave it covered for 20 minutes, then turn the fish. Return the lid and cook for a further 10 minutes, or until the internal temperature of the fish is 58°C (136°F).

Smoked trout with celeriac and spring onion remoulade

133

AIOLI

2 egg yolks

3 teaspoons Dijon mustard

2 confit garlic cloves (see recipe opposite)

1 small garlic clove

1 teaspoon white wine vinegar

pinch of salt

zest and juice of ½ lemon

270 ml (9 fl oz) vegetable oil

2½ tablespoons olive oil

pepper, to taste

1. In a food processor, blend the egg yolks, mustard, confit garlic, garlic, vinegar, salt and lemon juice.

2. Combine the two oils. Slowly and steadily pour the oil into the yolk mix while blending, until the mixture emulsifies and thickens. Season with a bit more salt and pepper to taste, then store in the fridge for up to a week.

CONFIT GARLIC

Everyone has those few garlic cloves that sprout in the fruit bowl, so before they get to that point, you can gently cook them and store them in oil. This brings out the sweetness of the garlic and preserves it for a whole range of uses. Confit garlic flavour is mild and earthly, ideal for salad dressings, sauces and even spreading on toast topped with fresh tomatoes. The confit oil is also handy for dressing cooked vegetables and meats.

WHAT YOU'LL NEED
- sterilised jar (see page 21)

500 g (1 lb 2 oz) garlic cloves, unpeeled

500 ml (17 fl oz/2 cups) olive oil

250 ml (8½ fl oz/1 cup) vegetable oil

1. Add the garlic and oils to a small pot and slowly heat over a low heat. Gently cook for 35–40 minutes, or until the cloves are soft when pressed with a spoon. Do not fry the garlic, otherwise it becomes chewy. If it begins to bubble, take it off the heat and let the oil cool slightly before returning to the stove on a lower heat.

2. Store the garlic in the oil in a sterilised jar in a cool, dry place or in the fridge, and use when needed. It is best eaten within 6 months.

Smoked trout with celeriac and spring onion remoulade

14

Sauerkraut soup with fromage blanc

Even if your grandparents didn't cook this soup for you, you could easily believe that they did. It's comforting and nourishing, and you'll make it so many times it'll bring feelings of nostalgia too.

SERVES 4

3 tablespoons grapeseed oil

2 onions, sliced

4 garlic cloves, sliced

1 bay leaf

300 g (10½ oz) Sauerkraut
(see page 143)

1½ litres (51 fl oz/6 cups) chicken
stock

juice of ½ lemon

150 g (5½ oz) Fromage blanc
(see page 143)

finely chopped chives, to serve

1. Heat the oil in a medium pot over a medium heat. Add the onions, garlic and bay leaf and cook for 15–20 minutes, or until they begin to soften and turn translucent.

2. Stir in the sauerkraut and cook for 5 minutes, then add the chicken stock. Bring the soup to a simmer, then turn the heat down to low and gently cook for 20 minutes, stirring occasionally.

3. Remove the pot from the heat and let sit for a few minutes, then stir through the lemon juice and fromage blanc. Serve topped with the chives.

SAUERKRAUT

Sauerkraut is the best way to discover fermentation. It's easy to see how the texture and flavour of cabbage change over time when you add salt. When you've made sauerkraut a few times, you're likely to want to try to ferment other ingredients – it's a confidence booster. Fermentation can be the solution for excess produce and limiting food waste.

WHAT YOU'LL NEED
• sterilised jar (see page 21)

1 head of cabbage, finely sliced, one large outer leaf reserved

2.5% of the weight of the cabbage in fine salt (see page 21)

1. Add the cabbage and salt to a bowl and rigorously press the salt into the cabbage until liquid begins to be drawn out. The cabbage will start to look translucent and there will be a generous amount of liquid. Cut a circle from the reserved cabbage leaf.

2. Press the salted cabbage into a sterilised jar, cover with the cabbage leaf and press it down until it's coved by liquid. Top the jar with a fermentation cap or a loosely fitted lid, and leave it to ferment at room temperature for 2 weeks. If you're not using a fermentation cap, open the jar daily to release the build-up of gas. This will prevent messy explosions. The cabbage will taste tangy and cheesy when fermented. Store in the fridge until ready to use. It will keep for up to 12 months.

FROMAGE BLANC

This is the first 'proper' cheese I learnt to make, thanks to my friend Colin Wood who came and worked with us at Oakridge for a few months. I watched him experiment and test cheese recipes, and he generously shared his knowledge with the kitchen team. That time spent together over hot pots of milk allowed my curiosity to grow, and I'm forever thankful. The style of fromage blanc highlights the subtleties of milk. It's creamy, salty and acidic. It will take two to three days to make, depending on how dense you want the consistency (I like it soft and spreadable), and make sure

to sterilise all the equipment. Cheesemaking ingredients and equipment can be bought at specialty stores and online.

WHAT YOU'LL NEED
• cheese measuring spoon
• syringe
• muslin or cheese cloth
• sterilised jars or container (see page 21)
• thermometer

2 litres (68 fl oz/8 cups) unhomogenised milk

1 drop on a cheese measuring spoon of Flora Danica mesophilic aromatic culture

1.3 ml calf rennet

fine salt

1. In a pot over a low heat, heat the milk to 85°C (185°F), gently stirring to prevent the milk from catching. Cool the milk to 30°C (86°F). I do this by submerging the pot in a sink of cold water.

2. Sprinkle the Flora Danica across the surface of the milk and allow it to hydrate for 1 minute then stir it through. Cover the pot and leave it for 30 minutes to allow the stater to inoculate the milk.

3. Check the milk is still at 30°C (86°F) and if it isn't, gently heat it back up to temperature.

4. Add the rennet while gently stirring the milk in a circular up-and-down motion. Only stir a few times to incorporate the rennet, then cover the pot and leave it to sit undisturbed overnight while the curd develops. If the milk is moved, the curd can break and stop developing.

5. The following day, line a strainer with a piece of cheese cloth or a clean tea towel and sit the strainer over a large bowl. Scoop the set curd into the strainer and allow the whey to drain. Fold the overhanging cloth or towel over the curds and place the bowl in the fridge overnight. You may need to empty the whey from the bowl a few times as the curds drain.

6. The following day, weigh the curd and add 2% of the weight of the curd in salt (see page 21). Stir the salt through the curd. The fromage blanc is ready to use and can be stored in a sterilised jar or container in the fridge for 2–3 weeks.

15

Rooster broth with buckwheat noodles and pickled mushrooms

Although eggs are my favourite ingredient, generally the egg and poultry industry is a brutal world. Male chickens are of no use, and if they don't go to the pet food industry, they are often discarded. Roosters are lean animals with a potentially 'strong' flavour compared to full-breasted meat birds, which means they carry some stigma. Their bones are harder, flavoursome and full of calcium; perfect for making broth. Some of the classic dishes such as coq au vin are made from roosters.

SERVES 4

340 g (12 oz) Buckwheat noodles, blanched (see page 151)

120 g (4½ oz) Pickled mushrooms (see recipe opposite)

300 g (10½ oz) watercress, picked

1.6 litres (54 fl oz) Rooster bone broth (see recipe opposite)

3 cm (1¼ in) piece of ginger, julienned

2 spring onions (scallions), finely sliced

soy sauce, to taste

brown rice vinegar, to taste

salt, to taste

Chilli oil (see page 73), to serve

1. Evenly divide the noodles, mushrooms and watercress between four serving bowls.

2. Bring the broth to a simmer over a medium heat and add the ginger and spring onion. Season the broth with the soy sauce, brown rice vinegar and salt to taste. Pour the hot broth over the noodles and finish with a drizzle of chilli oil before serving.

ROOSTER BONE BROTH

1 rooster
2 onions, chopped
1 garlic bulb, halved
6 spring onions (scallions), roughly chopped
80 g (2¾ oz) ginger, sliced
3 tablespoons apple cider vinegar
pinch of whole black peppercorns

1. Add all the ingredients to a large pot and add 7 litres (1½ gallons) of cold water. Bring the pot to a simmer over a medium heat, then turn off the heat and let it sit for 15 minutes.

2. Remove the rooster from the pot, pick the meat off the bones and return the bones to the pot. The meat can be refrigerated and used later in the soup if desired or alternatively I like to use it in sandwiches or salads.

3. Gently simmer the stock for 4 hours, skimming occasionally to remove any scum from the surface.

4. Drain the stock through a sieve, discarding the bones and vegetables. The stock will keep in the fridge for up to 1 week and in the freezer for up to 3 months.

PICKLED MUSHROOMS

Sweet pickling liquid works best with subtly flavoured ingredients. In this recipe it's poured over the raw mushrooms when hot to achieve the ideal texture.

WHAT YOU'LL NEED
- sterilised jar (see page 21)

300 g (10½ oz) shimeji mushrooms
¼ teaspoon Sichuan peppercorns
¼ teaspoon coriander seeds
1 star anise
½ cinnamon quill

PICKLING LIQUID

1 tablespoon tamari
350 ml (12 fl oz) white wine vinegar
45 g (1½ oz) caster (superfine) sugar
3 teaspoons (15 g/½ oz) salt

1. For the pickling liquid, stir all the ingredients together with 400 ml (13½ fl oz) of water in a medium pot. Bring it to a gentle simmer over a low–medium heat and cook, stirring, until the sugar has dissolved.

2. Break the mushrooms into small bundles and place them in a sterilised jar with the spices. Pour the hot pickling liquid over the mushrooms, leaving 1–2 cm (½–¾ in) of space at the top. Cut a circle of baking paper and place it over the surface of the mushrooms to keep them submerged. Fit the lid, then cool to room temperature. The pickle will keep for up to 12 months in the fridge.

Rooster broth with buckwheat noodles and pickled mushrooms

BUCKWHEAT NOODLES

Buckwheat is an extremely fast-growing and productive crop. It was one of the star performers at futurefoodsystem. I could harvest the grain only six weeks after planting, and I made breads, vegan sausages, teas and risotto. The best results, though, came with these noodles. Buckwheat is gluten-free and produces a gel-like enzyme that helps with binding. This means buckwheat dough can be rolled through a pasta machine immediately after mixing and be blanched straight away – there is no resting period required. Instant noodles.

WHAT YOU'LL NEED
• pasta machine

220 g (8 oz/1⅓ cups) buckwheat flour, plus extra for dusting

½ teaspoon fine salt

2 eggs

1 egg yolk

1. Combine the flour, salt, eggs and egg yolk in a medium bowl. Use the tips of your fingers to work the eggs into the flour until it resembles breadcrumbs. Squeeze the dough together and knead to form a smooth dough.

2. Divide the dough into two even pieces and flatten them into rectangles ready to feed through the pasta machine. (If you do not have a pasta machine, you can use a rolling pin and a knife).

3. Bring a medium pot of water to the boil.

4. Meanwhile, dust the dough with a bit of flour and feed it through the pasta machine on the widest setting. Decrease the setting and turn the dough 90 degrees before feeding it through again. Fold the sheet in thirds. Increase setting to the widest setting, turn the dough 90 degrees and feed the dough back through. Do this a few of times to work the dough.

5. Once you've got a nice, smooth dough, decrease the width by one setting, and roll through the dough. Continue to roll the dough, decreasing the width each time, until you have a thin sheet about 1½–2 mm (³⁄₆₄–¹⁄₁₆ in) thick. Cut the sheet into 30 cm (12 in) lengths, then run the sheet through the spaghetti cutter setting.

6. Cook the noodles, a handful or two at a time, plunging them straight into the boiling water for 15 seconds, stirring to prevent any noodles sticking together, then drain and coat with olive oil to stop them from sticking together.

7. The blanched noodles will last two days in a container in the fridge. I recommend using them in the rooster broth shortly after blanching them for the best results.

Rooster broth with buckwheat noodles and pickled mushrooms

16

Fried sardines with roasted almonds, skordalia and parsley salad

When it comes to fish, there are sustainable alternatives people can feel happy about consuming. We should consider buying small varieties of fish like sardines, which are fast-growing, abundant and high in omega-3 fatty acids. Masses of wild-caught small fish are being collected and turned into fish feed for larger species of farmed fish. At futurefoodsystem we made fish feed from algae, crickets and compost for our aquaponics systems.

SERVES 4

vegetable oil, for frying

8 sardines, butterflied

salt and pepper, to season

lemon wedges, to serve

SKORDALIA

700 g (1 lb 9 oz) potatoes, halved or quartered

6 small garlic cloves

90 ml (3 fl oz) olive oil, plus extra for drizzling

2 tablespoons apple cider vinegar

60 g (2 oz/⅓ cup) almonds, roasted and roughly chopped

zest and juice of 1 lemon

salt, to taste

PARSLEY SALAD

1 small shallot, very thinly sliced

salt

1 bunch flat-leaf (Italian) parsley, leaves picked

1. To make the scordalia, place the potatoes in cold, salted water in a pot and bring it to a gentle simmer. Cook for about 12–15 minutes or until tender and cooked through.

2. Strain the potatoes and return them to the pot. Grate the garlic into the hot potatoes using a microplane and add the olive oil, apple cider vinegar, almonds, and lemon zest and juice. Stir and season with salt to taste. The potatoes will break up slightly, which is desired, but don't overmix or they will turn gluey.

3. To make the parsley salad, rinse the shallot in cold, salted water (salty like the sea) and dry it. This removes any bitterness, keeps it crisp and seasons it. Mix the shallots with the parsley in a bowl and set aside.

4. Heat the oil in a frying pan over a medium heat. Season the skin-side of the sardines with salt and pepper. Lay the fish skin-side down into the hot frying pan. Cook until the flesh-side is warm to touch and you can see the sides of the fish have cooked, about 1–2 minutes. Turn and cook for a further 30 seconds then remove from the frying pan.

5. Serve the sardines topped with the parsley salad and drizzled with olive oil, with skordalia on the side, drizzled with olive oil. Serve the lemon wedges separately.

17

Murray cod with fennel salad and marinated vegetable dressing

Murray cod is a freshwater fish and the texture and fat content of the sweet, white, flaky flesh produces quality results when served raw, pan-seared, steamed and poached. In terms of quality, it presents a serious challenge to ocean fish, and it can be sustainably farmed.

SERVES 4

4 × 160–200 g (5½–7 oz) Murray cod fillets, skin on

salt

1 tablespoon vegetable oil

FENNEL SALAD

1 fennel bulb, thinly sliced, fronds picked and reserved

1 bunch flat-leaf (Italian) parsley, leaves picked

1 bunch basil, leaves picked

MARINATED VEGETABLE DRESSING

1½ tablespoon Red wine vinegar (see page 165)

Preserved vegetables (8–10 cherry tomatoes, 1 bullhorn pepper and 1 garlic clove), torn, plus 3 tablespoons of the marinade oil (see page 165)

1 tablespoon capers

½ teaspoon salt

1. Lay the fish skin-side up on paper towel on a plate and leave it, uncovered, in the fridge overnight to dry out the skin.

2. To make the salad, toss the ingredients together in a bowl.

3. To make the dressing, mix all the ingredients together in a small bowl.

4. Lightly salt the skin of the cod. Add the oil and the cod, skin-side down, to a cold pan. Cook over low–medium heat for 5–7 minutes, or until the flesh begins to turn white. The skin will begin to fry and turn crisp as the temperature increases. Once the skin is crisp and the flesh on top is warm to the touch, turn and cook for a further 1–2 minutes. Dress the fennel salad with the marinated vegetable dressing and serve with the cod.

PRESERVED VEGETABLES

WHAT YOU'LL NEED
- 1 × 1.5 litre (51 fl oz/6 cups) wide-mouthed jar, sterilised (see page 21)
- thermometer

1 kg (2 lb 3 oz) cherry tomatoes

4 garlic cloves, skin on

3 bullhorn peppers

400 ml (13½ fl oz) olive oil, plus extra

400 ml (13½ fl oz) grapeseed oil

8–10 whole black peppercorns

4 sprigs thyme

½ sprig rosemary

1 sprig flat-leaf (Italian) parsley

3 sprigs basil

1. Preheat the oven to 220°C (430°F).

2. Lightly toss the cherry tomatoes, garlic cloves and bullhorn peppers in a small amount of olive oil, lay them in a single layer on a baking tray and roast them for 30 minutes, until blistered. Cool slightly then remove the skin and seeds from the peppers.

3. In a pot, heat the oils, peppercorns, thyme and rosemary to 50°C (122°F) over a low heat.

4. Fill the sterilised jar one-third of the way with the warm oil. Layer the roasted vegetables, parsley and basil in the jar and top with the remaining oil, making sure everything is completely submerged. Fit the lid and keep at room temperature for two days then store in the fridge. It will keep for years.

RED WINE VINEGAR

This recipe for making red wine vinegar is similar to the process of making yoghurt (see page 53). A small amount of active vinegar mother is added to the red wine and then it's left to do its thing. It is best to use wine that has been opened for a number of days. This allows any sulphur to evaporate, which can prevent the wine from turning into vinegar. If you are using natural or minimal intervention wines this step is not necessary.

MAKES 750 ML (25½ FL OZ/3 CUPS)

WHAT YOU'LL NEED
- wide-mouthed jar, sterilised (see page 21)

125 ml (4 fl oz/½ cup) leftover red wine

375 ml (12½ fl oz/1½ cups) apple cider vinegar with active mother

1. Place the wine into the sterilised jar. Add the apple cider vinegar and cover the jar with a cloth so it's able to breathe. Leave at room temperature for 6 weeks to turn to vinegar, swirling the jar every couple of days to promote activity. After a few weeks, a 'jellyfish looking' disc will appear. This is a vinegar mother and is produced naturally. At this point the vinegar can be stored in the jar for years, but if you want to make more, leave a small amount of vinegar and the mother in the jar, add any leftover wine to the jar, cover and continue to brew for 6 weeks to make the next batch.

Murray cod with fennel salad and marinated vegetable dressing

18

Venison and red wine pie

I've never met a person who doesn't love a pie. I think the secret is crisp pastry – sturdy but not too thick – and a full-flavoured filling.

Deer are running rampant in Australia and considered an invasive species, with government-controlled culling programs in place to control their numbers. However, they are also free-range, organic and a delicious protein. Many Australians are not familiar with cooking and eating wild game meats, or their only dining experience may be limited to a seared underdone fillet. A bit boring.

Tender, slow-cooked dishes are a delicious alternative for presenting game meats, especially when they're wrapped in pastry.

SERVES 6–8

2 tablespoons vegetable oil

1.5 kg (3 lb 5 oz) venison shoulder or shank, sinew removed, cut into 2½ cm (1 in) cubes

1 brown onion, roughly diced

6 banana shallots, roughly diced

3 thyme sprigs

1 bay leaf

3 teaspoons black peppercorns, crushed

600 ml (20½ fl oz) red wine

200 g (7 oz) diced tomatoes or Tomato sugo (see page 181)

500 ml (17 fl oz/2 cups) vegetable stock

2 tablespoons cornflour (cornstarch)

30 g (1 oz) butter

salt, to taste

1 × quantity Rough puff pastry (see page 173)

EGG WASH

1 egg

2 tablespoons milk

pinch of salt

1. Heat 1 tablespoon of the oil in a medium pot over a high heat and sear the venison in batches until golden brown on all sides. Set aside.

2. Heat the remaining 1 tablespoon of oil in a pot over a medium heat. Add the onion, shallot, thyme, bay leaf and peppercorns and cook for 10 minutes, or until the onions are tender.

3. Add the venison, deglaze the pot with the red wine and cook for 5 minutes, then add the tomatoes and vegetable stock. Cook for 30–40 minutes at a gentle simmer or until the venison is tender.

4. Mix the cornflour with 70 ml of water in a small bowl to make a slurry. Add the slurry to the pot and stir through to thicken the sauce. Add the butter and season with salt. Refrigerate until the mixture is completely cool and you are ready to assemble the pie.

5. Lightly grease and line the bottom of a 25 × 3 cm (10 × 1¼ in) pie tin.

6. To make the egg wash, add all the ingredients to a small bowl and whisk to combine, then strain the mixture. It can be stored in an airtight container in the fridge for up to 1 week.

7. To assemble the pie, place one of the discs of pastry onto a lightly floured bench. Flour the surface and roll it out to a 3 mm (⅛ in) thick circle, about 45–48 cm (18–19 in) in diameter. Set aside and repeat with the second pastry disc. Line the pie tin with one of the pastry circles, leaving any excess pastry overhanging.

8. Fill the pie tin with the filling, spreading it evenly. Brush the edges of the pastry with egg wash, then lay the second circle over the filling. Press the edges of the pastry together to seal the pie, then cut away any excess pastry. Brush the surface with egg wash and use the tip of a knife to poke a steam hole in the centre of the pastry. Refrigerate, freeze or bake the pie.

9. To bake the pie, preheat the oven to 180°C (360°F) and bake for 35–40 minutes, or until the pastry is golden and cooked through and the filling is hot. Serve with a side salad or steamed vegetables.

ROUGH PUFF PASTRY

3 teaspoons white vinegar
625 g (1 lb 6 oz/3¾ cups) plain (all-purpose) flour
220 g (8 oz) butter, cubed
1 teaspoon salt

1. Mix the vinegar with 200 g (7 oz) cold water in a bowl and set aside.

2. Add the flour, butter and salt to a bowl and pinch the butter into the flour until it resembles rough breadcrumbs.

3. Add the water and vinegar mix to the flour and bring it together with your hands to form a dough. Do not overwork the dough; it's fine to see streaks of butter. Divide the dough into two even pieces. Press each piece into a disc, wrap and refrigerate until ready to use. The pastry will keep in the fridge for up to 1 week and can be stored in the freezer for up to 3 months; thaw it in the fridge before use.

19

Stuffed rainbow chard with olives, capers and preserved lemon in tomato sugo

In this recipe large chard leaves are used like cannoli wrappers to encase flavoured rice and then baked with bottled summer tomatoes. Adding the preserved fruits seasons and brightens the dish.

SERVES 4

1 cup short grain rice

olive oil, for frying and drizzling

1 onion, roughly chopped

4 garlic cloves, roughly chopped

6–8 large rainbow chard leaves

100 g (3½ oz /¼ cup) pitted green olives, roughly chopped

1 tablespoon capers, roughly chopped

50 g (1¾ oz/⅓ cup) whole roasted almonds, roughly chopped

handful of basil leaves, roughly chopped

½ teaspoon dried oregano

1 teaspoon diced zest of Preserved lemons (see page 181)

juice of 1 lemon

1 litre (34 fl oz/4 cups) Tomato sugo (see page 181)

parmesan or mozzarella (optional)

1. Rinse the rice under cold running water and place it in a small pot with 375 ml (12½ fl oz/1½ cups) of water. Bring to a simmer over a medium–high heat, cover the pot and turn the heat down to the lowest setting. Cook for 14 minutes without removing the lid. Fluff the rice with a fork and leave it in the fridge to cool.

2. Preheat the oven to 180°C (360°F).

3. Heat a small amount of olive oil over a low–medium heat and gently cook the onion and garlic for 10 minutes, or until tender. Set aside.

4. Boil a medium pot of water and blanch the chard for 1 minute, then refresh in ice water. Squeeze the leaves dry then spread them flat, stem-side down, on a chopping board or kitchen bench.

5. Combine the olives, capers, almonds and basil in a bowl. Add the cooled rice, onion mix, oregano, preserved lemon, lemon juice and a drizzle of olive oil. Stir to combine.

6. Place a large spoon of the rice mix at the base of a blanched leaf, closest to the stem, and roll the leaf over the mix, folding in the overhanging edges and rolling down the length of the leaf to form a sealed parcel. Place the parcel in a baking dish, seam-side down, and repeat with the remaining leaves and filling.

7. Cover the parcels with the tomato sugo and top with cheese, if using. Bake for 30–40 minutes, or until the leaves are tender and the filling is hot. Serve with a side salad.

TOMATO SUGO

Tomato sugo is the workhorse of the kitchen. This method can be used with tomatillos, eggplants (aubergines) or capsicums (bell peppers). The aim is to cook out the excess liquid from the fruit or vegetable, add salt and sugar then bottle it hot in sterilised jars for a long shelf life.

MAKES 1.7–2 LITRES (57–68 FL OZ/7-8 CUPS)

WHAT YOU'LL NEED
- 2 × 1-litre (34 fl oz/4 cups) bottles, sterilised (see page 21)

100 ml (3½ fl oz) olive oil	
4 onions, roughly diced	
½ teaspoon dried oregano	
4 kg (8 lb 13 oz) tomatoes, roughly diced	
4 teaspoons caster (superfine) sugar	
3 teaspoons (15 g/½ oz) salt	
2 basil sprigs	

1. Heat the olive oil in a large pot over a medium heat. Add the onions and oregano and cook for 15–20 minutes, or until tender. Turn the heat down to low and add the tomatoes. Cook for 30–40 minutes or until most of the liquid has evaporated, stirring occasionally to prevent the sauce from burning.

2. Add the sugar and salt and cook for a further 10 minutes. The tomato sauce will thicken and become glossy when ready to bottle.

3. Pour the hot mix into sterilised bottles. Insert a basil sprig into each bottle, then cap and allow to cool to room temperature. The sugo will last for up to 12 months unopened. Once opened, store in the fridge for up to a week.

PRESERVED LEMONS

Dry salting lemons draws out the moisture and creates a brine that preserves the fruit and inhibits harmful bacteria growth. The acidity of the lemon disappears and you're left with an intense flora note. The zest of the lemon is what you want to use once the fruit has been completely preserved. It will feel soft when pinched between your fingers and will have changed colour to a deeper yellow. Remove the flesh from the rind and gently rinse under water. I like to use the zest in dressings, salads, pastas and for my stuffed rainbow chard.

WHAT YOU'LL NEED
- 2½ litre (85 fl oz/10 cups) sterilised jar (see page 21)

8 lemons, plus extra lemon juice if needed	
about 400 g (14 oz) salt	
1½ teaspoons coriander seeds	
3 bay leaves (preferably fresh)	

1. Cut the lemons into quarters lengthways most of the way through (about three quarters) so each one is still intact at the base. Mix the salt, coriander seeds and bay leaves.

2. Press some of the salt into the cuts in each lemon. Sprinkle more salt into the base of the sterilised jar, then squeeze the salted lemons into the jar. Sprinkle more salt over each lemon as you stack them. The salt will draw out the juice and fill the jar, but you can add more juice to cover the lemons if needed. Secure the lid and leave the jar on the kitchen bench. Each day for the first week, invert the jar to redistribute the salt from the top to the bottom. The lemons will be ready to use after 6 weeks and will last for 12 months. Store the lemons in the fridge after opening.

Stuffed rainbow chard with olives, capers and preserved lemon in tomato sugo

20

Red
pepper
pasta

This might be the simplest dish in the book but one of the best. It requires only two simple processes: roasting, fermenting and blending the peppers; and making the pasta. The peppers are fermented ahead of time, and the pasta can also be made ahead and either dried or frozen. This dish can be prepared in the same amount of time it takes to order food from a delivery service. Good food can be simple, efficient and delicious.

SERVES 4

300 g (10½ oz) Fermented red peppers (see page 189), or roasted preserved peppers

1 × quantity Rye pasta (see page 189)

100 g (3½ oz) unsalted butter

juice of 1 lemon

basil leaves, to serve

1. Boil and salt a large pot of water for cooking the pasta. Blend the peppers until smooth.

2. Add the peppers to a large pan over a medium heat. As the pepper puree begins to heat through, add the pasta to the pot of boiling water and cook for 2 minutes.

3. Once the pasta is al dente, drain it and toss it through the sauce with the butter and lemon juice. Serve topped with torn basil leaves.

RYE PASTA

WHAT YOU'LL NEED
• pasta machine

120 g (4½ oz/⅔ cups) rye grains, freshly milled (see page 97)

160 g (5½ oz/1 cup) 00 flour

½ teaspoon salt

1 egg

2 egg yolks

1. Combine the flours and salt. Add the egg, egg yolks and 3 tablespoons of water and mix to form a smooth, elastic dough. Flatten the dough into a disc, wrap and refrigerate for at least 30 minutes.

2. Dust the dough with a bit of flour and feed it through the pasta machine on the widest setting. Decrease the setting and turn the dough 90 degrees before feeding it through again. Fold the sheet in thirds. Increase setting to the widest setting, turn the dough 90 degrees and feed the dough back through. Do this a few times to work the dough. Once you've got a nice, smooth, elastic dough, decrease the width by one setting, and roll through the dough. Continue rolling the dough, decreasing the width each time, until you have a thin sheet about 2 mm (1/16 in) thick, then use a knife to cut it into pappardelle, about 2 cm (¾ in) wide.

3. Lay the pasta on a floured tray or hang it to dry while you repeat this process with the remaining portions. You can store the pasta in an airtight container in the freezer, with the layers separated by sheets of baking paper, for up to 3 weeks. Alternatively, you can dry it completely and store it for up to a week in an airtight container in the pantry.

FERMENTED RED PEPPERS

I've always been reluctant to do anything to capsicums – it seems a shame to take away the sweet juicy crunch of the flesh by cooking them – but fermenting them changed my opinion. It's incredible what a single fermented pepper can bring to a dish. Their sweetness combined with the charred, blistered flesh and the salt and tang of fermentation can elevate even the simplest dish.

WHAT YOU'LL NEED
• 1-litre (34 fl oz/4 cups) jar, sterilised (see page 21)

6 large red capsicums (bell peppers)

oil, for brushing

1.5% of the weight of the prepared capsicums in fine salt (see page 21)

1. Preheat the oven to 220°C (430°F) and line a baking tray with baking paper.

2. Lightly coat the outsides of the capsicums with a thin layer of oil, place them on the tray and bake for 30 minutes or until the skin is charred and blistered. Set them aside until they're cool enough to handle.

3. Peel away the skin and remove the seeds. Weigh the flesh and add 1.5% salt.

4. Place the capsicum in a sterilised jar, cover with a piece of cloth and leave it at room temperature for 2–3 days to ferment. The peppers will begin to bubble and fizz when they start to ferment. At this point, add the lid and place the jar in the fridge to slow and stop the fermentation. The fermented capsicums will keep for up to 6 months.

21

Sprout
risotto

This is a tasty, nutritious vegan risotto. Sprouting grains and pulses activates enzymes that turn the starch into sugar, which makes the nutrients more available for the plant or, in our case, for our bodies to digest. You'll need to start this recipe a couple of days in advance to allow time for the grains and pulses to sprout.

SERVES 4

50 g (1¾ oz) brown rice

50 g (1¾ oz) dried chickpeas

50 g (1¾ oz) dried de puy lentils

50 g (1¾ oz) dried mung beans

50 g (1¾ oz) dried green lentils

1 tablespoon olive oil

1 shallot, diced

400 ml (13½ fl oz) mushroom or vegetable stock

4 tablespoons Cashew cream (see recipe opposite), or Cashew and fenugreek cream (see page 39)

120 ml (4 fl oz/¼ cup) Spinach puree (see below)

1 tablespoon brown rice vinegar

salt

pinch of ground black pepper

juice of ½ lemon

SPINACH PUREE

1 bunch English spinach (approximately 220 g / 8 oz)

1 tablespoon vegetable oil

1. Sprout the grains and pulses according to the method on page 39. This will take several days.

2. Once the sprouts are ready, heat the oil in a pot over a medium heat. Add the shallot and cook for 6 minutes, or until tender. Heat the mushroom stock in a separate pot.

3. Add the rice to the shallot and cook, stirring, for a minute to coat the rice in oil, then pour in the mushroom stock. Simmer for 12–15 minutes, or until the rice is just tender.

4. Meanwhile, to make the spinach puree, bring a large pot of water to the boil over a high heat and fill a large bowl with ice water. Blanch the spinach leaves for 20 seconds in the boiling water, then immediately refresh them in the ice water. Drain the spinach and squeeze out any excess water, then blend it with the oil and 3 tablespoons of water until completely smooth. Set aside. The puree can be stored in an airtight container in the fridge for up to 1 week or stored in the freezer for up to 3 months.

5. Add the remaining grains and pulses to the rice, bring it back to a simmer and cook for 2–3 minutes, then add the cashew cream. Add the spinach puree and season with lemon juice, brown rice vinegar, salt and pepper to taste.

CASHEW CREAM

150 g (5½ oz) cashew nuts

2½ tablespoons vegetable oil

1. Blend the cashews, oil and 150 ml (5 fl oz) water in a blender until completely smooth. Store in an airtight container in the fridge for up to 1 week, or store in the freezer for up to 3 months.

22

Roast potatoes with macadamia pesto

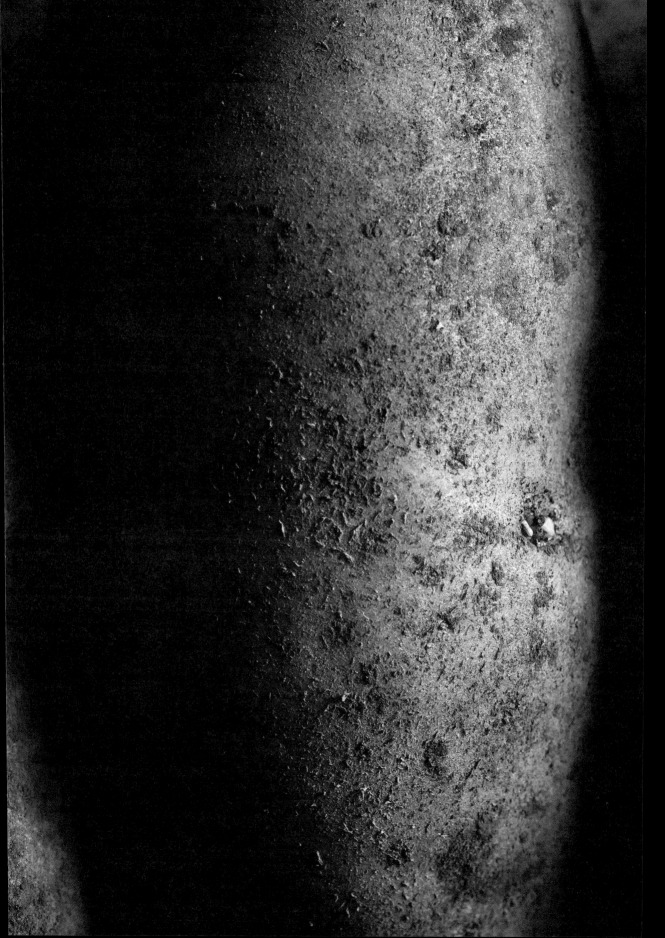

This side dish always makes me think of my friend and fellow chef Louise Daily, who is the master of the green sauce – give her a bunch of herbs and she'll produce something incredible. I'd now make this over traditional pesto any day – it's balanced, mellow and moreish. Besides tossing it over roasted potatoes, you can use it as a dip, in pasta or as a condiment.

SERVES 4 AS A SIDE

1 kg (2 lb 3 oz) potatoes, cut into even-sized pieces

3–4 tablespoons vegetable oil

salt flakes, to season

325 g (11½ oz/1 cup approximately) Macadamia pesto (see page 203)

¼ lemon

1. Preheat the oven to 180°C (360°F) and line a baking tray with grease-proof paper.

2. Spread the potatoes evenly over the tray, lightly drizzle with oil and season with a couple of pinches of salt. Roast the potatoes in the oven for 25 minutes, or until golden brown and tender.

3. Place the roasted potatoes in a medium bowl and gently fold through the pesto to coat, being careful not to break the potatoes. Season with a squeeze of lemon juice and salt to taste, then serve.

MACADAMIA PESTO

This isn't a traditional pesto. It's made with macadamia nuts and the recipe doesn't use any cheese, making it a vegan version. However, it is just as satisfying, and I find it has a lighter, less dominating flavour, making it more versatile. It's great with pasta, as a dip, as a condiment and on eggs. I also love it on potatoes as a side dish.

250 g (9 oz) macadamia nuts

250 ml (8½ fl oz/1 cup) vegetable oil

1 bunch basil, stalks and leaves

1 bunch flat-leaf (Italian) parsley, tender stalks and leaves

2 garlic cloves

150 ml (5 fl oz) olive oil

2 teaspoons sherry vinegar

zest and juice of 1 lemon

generous pinch of salt

pepper, to taste

1. Preheat the oven to 170°C (340°F).

2. Roast the macadamias on a tray in the oven for 7 minutes, or until golden brown, then set aside to cool.

3. Once cool, blend the nuts into a fine crumble in a food processor then transfer them to a medium bowl.

4. Blend the vegetable oil, herbs and garlic to a fine paste.

5. Scrape the herb paste into the bowl with the nuts, and add the olive oil, sherry vinegar and lemon zest and juice. Stir to combine, and season with salt and pepper to taste. The pesto will keep for 1 month in an airtight container in the fridge.

Roast potatoes with macadamia pesto

23

Brussels sprouts and bacon with mushroom XO

I've had people tell me they hate brussels sprouts and then demolish this dish. Matt Stone, our fellow chef Harry and I travelled to Hong Kong one year to cook at the Hong Kong Jockey Club. It was a prestigious invitation, and we were all very excited. At the time we were making XO sauce with dried smoked trout at Oakridge and we decided to use it on our week-long Hong Kong menu. As a rule at Oakridge, we didn't use any seafood in our cooking, so farmed river trout was a fitting substitute. It didn't occur to me until we were setting up for our first dinner service that we were serving 'XO' that wasn't really XO in the place it had originated. It was too late to change the wording on the menu and I was worried about expectations as well as offending anyone. The dinner went on and towards the end of service the maître d' entered the kitchen asking how the XO had been made. I swallowed hard and thought, 'Here we go'. I was busy plating the last dishes when Matt started to portion the XO into jars. He turned to me with a puzzled grin and said, 'They love it, people want to take it home.' We both laughed. Over the week we gave away many jars of sauce, made 500 croissants and witnessed two typhoons. It's a trip I will never forget, and I am reminded of it every time I open a jar of XO.

SERVES 4 AS A SIDE

100 g (3½ oz) Bacon (see page 210), diced

500 g (1 lb 2 oz) brussels sprouts, halved

50 g (1¾ oz) unsalted butter

100 g (3½ oz) Mushroom XO (see recipe opposite)

1 teaspoon tamari

1 teaspoon brown rice vinegar

juice of ½ lemon

salt, to taste

1. Heat a pan over a medium heat and cook the bacon for 5 minutes, or until the fat has rendered.

2. Place the brussels sprouts cut-side down in the pan with the bacon. Turn the heat down to low–medium and cook for 8–10 minutes, or until the brussels sprouts begin to caramelise.

3. Turn the brussels sprouts and increase the heat to medium, then add the butter to the pan. When the butter has melted, add the XO sauce and fry slightly, then season with the tamari, vinegar, lemon juice and salt. Serve once the brussels sprouts are tender and cooked through.

MUSHROOM XO

XO is a sauce traditionally made with dried shrimp, scallops and fish cooked with chilli, garlic and ginger. Originating from Hong Kong, it's used as a spicy condiment that's served with almost everything. This recipe is far from traditional, and I usually make it in autumn during mushroom season and replace the dried seafood with pine or field mushrooms. Cost effective and with an amazing texture, it's a good way to preserve a large amount of mushrooms.

MAKES 2 LITRES (68 FL OZ/8 CUPS)

WHAT YOU'LL NEED
• sterilised jars (see page 21)

150 g (5½ oz) ginger, coarsely chopped	
200 g (7 oz) garlic cloves	
4 brown onions, coarsely chopped	
1 litre (34 fl oz/4 cups) oil	
1 kg (2 lb 3 oz) Fermented chilli (see recipe opposite)	
700 g (1 lb 9 oz) mushrooms, sliced	
tamari, to taste	
brown rice vinegar, to taste	

1. In a food processor blend the ginger, garlic and onion to a rough paste.

2. Heat the oil in a tall, large pot over a medium heat. Add the paste to the oil along with the fermented chilli. Stir to prevent the paste from sticking. The mixture will emulsify and the paste will bubble as it begins to cook. Turn the heat to low and cook, stirring occasionally, for 1–1½ hours or until the colour deepens and the oil splits completely from the paste.

3. Stir in the sliced mushrooms and cook for a further 45 minutes. Once the oil splits again from the chilli and the mushrooms are cooked through, the mixture is ready.

4. Season with a small amount of tamari and vinegar, or to taste. Portion the hot XO into sterilised jars, seal with the lids and let them cool to room temperature. Store in the fridge for up to 12 months.

FERMENTED CHILLI

Add fermented chilli to anything and everything that requires heat and added depth. The heat can be adjusted with a spoonful of honey or sugar if it's too hot to handle once fermented. Fermented chilli adds a layer of complexity to the Mushroom XO sauce.

WHAT YOU'LL NEED
• sterilised jars (see page 21)
• cloth to cover the jars

1 kg (2 lb 3 oz) long red chillies, halved lengthways, half deseeded
2% salt of the weight of deseeded blended chillies

1. Blend the chillies to a rough puree. Add a bit of water to help blend if needed.

2. Place the blended chillies in a bowl and stir through the salt, then divide the mixture between the sterilised jars. Cover the jars with the cloth, and leave them to ferment at room temperature for 4 days. The chillies will begin to bubble and fizz and a white mould may appear on the surface of the chillies. White mould is safe; simply remove it by scraping it off or stir it through.

3. After 4 days, add the lids and transfer the jars to the fridge to stop the fermentation. Fermented chilli will last for 3–6 months refrigerated.

BACON

Making bacon follows a similar process to making smoked trout (page 132), as the meat is cured in flavoured salt before it is smoked, but one major difference is time, as pork flesh is denser and takes longer to cure. In both cases the flesh is preserved in two ways: first with salt and then with smoke. Animal fat carries flavour, so fattier cuts of meat are better for curing and smoking. I use various woods and wood chips for smoking as well as bay leaf branches and thick rosemary branches. You can use regular salt in this recipe, however curing salt will keep the meat an appealing colour. Curing salts can be found at specialty stores and online.

WHAT YOU'LL NEED
- smoker or charcoal grill with a lid
- wood chips, soaked in water
- bay leaf branches and thick rosemary branches, soaked in water (optional)
- digital thermometer

1 × 2 kg (4 lb 6 oz) piece pork belly, skin on (wild boar belly is even better)

CURE

50 g (1¾ oz/2½ tablespoons) salt

1 teaspoon curing salt #2

4 strips of orange zest

½ teaspoon coriander seeds

1 bay leaf

½ teaspoon peppercorns

60 ml (2 fl oz/¼ cup) maple syrup

1. To make the cure, combine all the ingredients in a bowl.

2. Rub the cure all over the pork belly, place in a snug fitting container, cover and refrigerate. Every day for the following 8 days, turn the pork over and return it to the fridge.

3. On day 8, remove the pork from the fridge, rinse off the cure with water and pat it dry with a paper towel. Return the pork to the fridge overnight, uncovered, so the surface of the meat becomes tacky.

4. Smoke the bacon using one of the following methods.

How to hot smoke with a smoker

1. Preheat the smoker to 140–150 °C (285–300°F), then add the smoking chips or bay leaf branches to create smoke.

2. Hot smoke the pork belly for 25 minutes, turn and cook for a further 20–30 minutes to an internal temperature of 63–65 °C (145–149°F) on a digital thermometer.

3. Remove the bacon and allow it to rest and cool. It will last up to 2 weeks in the fridge or 3–4 months in the freezer.

How to hot smoke without a smoker

1. Light a coal grill and let it burn down to glowing coals. We are looking to create an environment of 140–150 °C (285–300°F) when the lid is on. Place the smoking chips or bay branches on the hot coals.

2. Place the pork belly on the grill rack and cover with the lid to trap the smoke. Leave it covered for 25 minutes, turn and cook for a further 20–30 minutes to an internal temperature of 63–65 °C (145–149°F) on a digital thermometer.

3. Remove the bacon and allow it to rest and cool. It will last up to 2 weeks in the fridge or 3–4 months in the freezer.

24

Ultimate
seed mix

This ultimate seed mix is all about texture. The texture of food holds as much importance to me as flavour, and our expectations of food are shaped by our past experiences, especially when it comes to texture. Biting into a soft floury apple is disappointing once you've enjoyed the crisp juicy fruit in its prime. We seek the crisp, crunch and crackle of food on a primal level. It's believed these textures relate to safe foods and higher nutrition. On the other hand, slimy textures can be an acquired taste – maybe that's because sliminess is often associated with food spoilage. Store this seed mix in a jar and use it to top salads, grilled vegetables, skewered meats, dips and soups. Sprinkle it like fairy dust.

MAKES 240 G (8½ OZ)

100 g (3½ oz/⅔ cups) pepitas (pumpkin seeds)

45 g (1½ oz/¼ cup) linseed (flaxseed)

15 g (½ oz/4 teaspoons) sesame seeds

20 g (¾ oz/2 tablespoons) hemp seeds

60 g (2 oz/¼ cup, heaped) buckwheat

1 teaspoon salt flakes

½ tablespoon dried oregano

½ teaspoon sumac

1. One variety at a time, toast the seeds and buckwheat in a dry pan over a medium heat until golden and place them in a bowl to cool. Season the toasted seeds with the salt, oregano and sumac.

2. Take a third of the seed mix and roughly blend to create a crumble. Stir the crumble back through the seed mix and let it cool completely. It will keep for 6 months in an airtight container in the cupboard.

25

Tigernut cake with preserved quince

Tigernut are not actually nuts; they're tubers in the same family as the potato. They are the size of hazelnuts and they grow at the base of a grass that's classified as a weed in some parts of Australia. I've never used such a versatile ingredient – they're gluten-, dairy- and nut-free, and because of their starch content and sweetness, they can be used as a replacement for sugar, flour and milk. High in protein and fibre and pretty much allergen-free, tigernuts are a valuable ingredient. You can bake seasonal fruits and berries like plums, strawberries and bananas into this cake. My favourite is preserved quince, because of its dense texture and light acidity. With little effort, tigernuts can also be transformed into custard and ice cream by blending the tuber with water and then cooking it over a low heat until it thickens. The thickened milk is sweet and creamy like custard and can then be churned into ice-cream. You can use tigernut flour in this recipe instead of blending whole nuts, but the cake will be denser and less sweet.

SERVES 12

240 g (8½ oz/1⅓ cups) dried tigernuts

140 g (5 oz) honey

3 eggs, separated

240 ml (8 fl oz) grapeseed oil, plus extra for greasing

1 × quantity Honey-cooked quinces (see page 225), each quarter cut into thirds

1. Preheat the oven to 180°C (360°F) and lightly oil and line the base of a shallow 20–22 cm (8–8¾ in) cake tin with baking paper.

2. Blend the tigernuts to a fine powder in a food processor or blender.

3. Whisk together the honey and egg yolks in a medium bowl to form a paste. Continue to whisk while slowly drizzling the oil into the yolk mix. The mixture will emulsify and start to look similar to a lemon curd.

4. Using a clean whisk and another bowl, whisk the egg whites to soft peaks. Fold the tigernut flour into the yolk mix, then gently fold through the egg whites, retaining as much air as possible.

5. Pour the mix into your lined cake tin and arrange the quince in a single layer on top. Bake for 30–35 minutes, or until a skewer comes out clean. Set aside for 10 minutes before removing from the tin.

HONEY-COOKED QUINCES

Preserving food in honey dates back to Egyptian times, and I'm curious to explore the possibilities. Quinces are considered inedible unless they're cooked or preserved. I like quince paste, but the amount of refined sugar required is a bit of a turn off for me. Cooking and preserving quince in honey was an exciting discovery. You can achieve a similar colour and consistency to quince paste and the bright flavour and shape of the fruit is retained.

750 g (1 lb 11 oz) honey

juice of 1 orange

4 large quinces, cored and quartered

1. Add the honey, orange juice and 450 ml (15 fl oz) of water to a wide, deep pan and stir to dissolve the honey, then arrange the quince quarters in a single layer in the pan.

2. Place the pan over a low-medium heat and gently simmer for 45 minutes. Turn the quinces and cook for a further 30–45 minutes, or until the quince turns a deep burgundy colour. The water will evaporate and the honey will candy the quince.

3. Gently remove the quince from the pan, transfer it to a container, pour the remaining liquid over the quince and let it cool. The quince will last for weeks in an airtight container in the fridge.

Tigernut cake with preserved quince

26

Layered lemon with granita, honey and yuzu curd

With only lemons for dessert, winter at futurefoodsystem was a challenge. Since we didn't use any refined sugar, flour, dairy or gelatine, balancing the zesty, sour fruit was a bit of a noodle scratcher. Lemon tarts, sorbets and puddings were all out of the question. I'm not going to lie: I panicked a bit. This dessert uses three types of preservation: freezing, curd and flavoured oils. These elements can be used individually, but when combined, they produce a beautifully simple yet sophisticated dessert.

SERVES 4

4 lemons

4 tablespoons Yuzu curd (see page 232)

4 teaspoons honey

1 × quantity Lemon granita (see page 232)

Geraldton wax leaves, finely chopped, for garnish

1. Cut a thin sliver of lemon off the bottom of each lemon, so the fruits can stand on their own, then cut the top off the lemons to expose the flesh, creating an opening big enough for a teaspoon to enter but still retaining the shape of the lemon. Remove the flesh and juice (use it to make the granita) and place the hollow lemons in the freezer for about 4 hours or overnight.

2. When ready to serve, fill the lemons in layers: start with a tablespoon of curd, then add a teaspoon of honey and top with lemon granita, filling each lemon to the top. Sprinkle with Geraldton wax leaves and serve immediately.

LEMON GRANITA

The key to freezing any fruit or vegetable is capturing the produce at its seasonal best and freezing the ingredient in a single layer as quickly as possible. Freeze the fruit in appropriate serving sizes in airtight containers to prevent ice crystals forming. Lemon juice also freezes well because it retains its original sour and zesty qualities when it is frozen.

---

juice of 4 lemons (about 200 ml/7 fl oz); use the juice from the hollowed-out lemons if making the Layered lemons on page 230)

---

20 g (¾ oz) raw (demerara) sugar, or 10% of the weight of juice (see page 21), optional

---

1. Add the lemon juice, sugar (if using) and 2½ tablespoons of water to a small bowl and stir until the sugar has dissolved. Freeze the liquid in a small container until completely solid, about 4 hours or overnight.

2. Run a fork across the surface of the frozen juice to break it up and return the granita to the freezer until ready to use. It will keep for up to 2 weeks.

YUZU CURD

Curds traditionally use eggs, sugar, citrus juice and butter and are pasteurised with heat to preserve the citrus flavour. In this recipe, sugar and dairy have been replaced with honey and a flavoured oil to create a similar texture, full flavour and to preserve the curd. I've used yuzu oil, which is acidic, bright and has a unique floral note. You can also use lemon, mandarin or orange oil.

---

4 egg yolks

---

60 g (2 oz/3 tablespoons) honey

---

1 tablespoon lemon juice

1½ tablespoons sparkling wine (white wine also works)

---

100 ml (3½ fl oz) yuzu oil or Flavoured citrus oil (see recipe opposite)

---

1. In a heatproof bowl, whisk the egg yolks, honey and lemon juice until combined.

2. Place the bowl over a slow simmering pot of water, making sure the bowl isn't touching the water. Add the sparkling wine and whisk vigorously until the mix begins to pale and thicken, then slowly drizzle in the yuzu or citrus oil and cook for 4–5 minutes, or until the curd has emulsified and become glossy and thick. Store in a sealed container and place in the fridge to cool.

3. Once cold, stir the curd to knock out the air bubbles and create a thick curd. Refrigerate until ready to use. The curd can be stored for up to a week and half in the fridge.

FLAVOURED CITRUS OIL

Flavoured oils are made by infusing oil with another ingredient that has a high concentration of natural oil. For example, lemons contain pungent oils within their skin, which can be seen when the skin is firmly squeezed. Heat the skin in olive or almond oil to extract and preserve its flavour.

WHAT YOU'LL NEED
• sterilised jar (see page 21)

peel of 2 lemons (or yuzu fruit, oranges or mandarins), pith removed

300 ml (10 fl oz) olive oil or almond oil

1. Remove any remaining pith from the lemon peel, leaving only the yellow skin. Place the peel in a heatproof bowl and add the oil. Place the bowl over a slow simmering pot of water, making sure the bowl isn't touching the water. Very gently heat the oil for 2 hours.

2. Strain the oil and pour it into a sterilised jar. It will last up to six months in the cupboard.

Layered lemon with granita, honey and yuzu curd

27

Plum galette with caccio ricotta

A galette is the quintessential expression of seasonal produce –
a blank canvas for both fruit and vegetables. This galette is topped with
bottled plums. Bottling and fermenting are two distinct preservation
methods. Fermenting produces funky flavour profiles by promoting
natural bacteria growth, and bottling inhibits bacteria growth by
using alcohol and sugar to create a sterile environment that captures
the original flavour of the ingredient. Unopened bottled fruit doesn't
require refrigeration.

SERVES 12

1 quantity Galette pastry (see
page 241)

6 Bottled plums (see page 241),
sliced

Caccio ricotta (see page 243),
to serve

pinch of caster (superfine) sugar

EGG WASH

1 egg

2 tablespoons milk

pinch of salt

1. Preheat the oven to 170°C (340°F).

2. For the egg wash, whisk all the ingredients in a bowl until well
   combined, then pass the mixture through a strainer.

3. On a floured surface, roll the pastry out to a 0.5 cm (0.2 in) thick
   circle, and arrange the plums on top, leaving 5 cm (2 in) of pastry
   around the edge. Fold the overhanging pastry over the plums,
   softly pressing it down. Brush the pastry with the egg wash and
   sprinkle it with a pinch of sugar. Bake for 35–40 minutes, or until
   golden and crisp on the underside.

4. Let the galette cool for 5 minutes before serving with a generous
   dollop of caccio ricotta.

GALETTE PASTRY

100 g (3½ oz) cold butter, diced (for a recipe see page 59)

240 g (8½ oz) plain (all-purpose) flour, plus extra for dusting

2 tablespoons caster (superfine) sugar

pinch of salt

1. Add butter and flour to a medium bowl and pinch the butter into the flour to create thin butter flakes that are evenly distributed throughout the flour.

2. Stir in the sugar and salt then add 120 ml (4 fl oz/½ cup) of cold water. Bring everything together to form a just-mixed dough with no dry lumps.

3. Press the dough into a disc, wrap it and leave it to rest in the fridge for 20–30 minutes. The dough will keep in the fridge for 1 week and in the freezer for up to 3 months.

BOTTLED PLUMS

WHAT YOU'LL NEED
• sterilised jar (see page 21)

8–10 plums, halved

500 ml (17 fl oz/2 cups) vodka or gin

250 g (9 oz/1 cup) caster (superfine) sugar

2 tablespoons white wine vinegar

2 green cardamom pods

1 cinnamon quill

1. Layer the plums in a sterilised jar, cut-side down and overlapping.

2. Heat the vodka, sugar and 700 ml (23½ fl oz) of water in a pot over a medium heat to 85°C (185°F), just before it starts to simmer. Remove it from the heat and add the vinegar, cardamom and cinnamon.

3. Pour the hot liquid over the plums to cover completely. Cover the jar with the lid while still hot and let it cool completely at room temperature. When sealed, the fruit will last up to 12 months. Refrigerate once open; the plums will keep for 6 months if you keep them submerged.

CACCIO RICOTTA

The difference between caccio ricotta and cooked milk ricotta is that caccio ricotta is heated milk set with rennet, a process that results in a creamy high-moisture cheese. Cooked milk ricotta is heated milk split with vinegar to separate the curds, typical of what you'd find at the store. Caccio ricotta is delicious sweetened with a little sugar and served with preserved fruit. This cheesemaking is relatively quick and includes my favourite process of setting and hooping curds.

WHAT YOU'LL NEED
- dosing syringe
- thermometer

2 litres (68 fl oz/8 cups) unhomogenised milk
1 ml rennet
caster (superfine) sugar, to taste

1. In a clean sterilised pot, heat the milk to 80°C (176°F) over a medium heat, continuously stirring so the milk doesn't catch. Remove the pot from the heat and let the milk cool to 38°C (100°F). This can be done by plunging the pot into a sink of cold water.

2. Once at temperature, take it off the heat and add the rennet, then stir 4–5 times to evenly distribute. Cover the pot and leave it undisturbed for 50 minutes for the curd to form.

3. Line a strainer with a clean tea towel and place the strainer over a bowl.

4. Check the milk has set by making a small shallow incision on the surface of the milk. Lift the incision – when it's a clean straight split the curd is ready. Scoop the curd into the strainer, fold the overhanging edges of the tea towel over the curd and place the bowl in the fridge for 4 hours for the curd to drain (if you prefer a denser, drier ricotta leave the curd to drain for longer).

5. Place the drained ricotta in a bowl, and add sugar to taste. Store in the fridge for up to a week.

28

Sponge cake with rhubarb and lemon myrtle jam

My nan was a brilliant home baker. She rescued over-ripe apricots and plums from Queen Victoria Market to make into jams, which meant that week we would be treated to mouth-watering apricot tea cakes, plum drop biscuits and coconut slice. She was a thrifty preserver of the seasons and taught me to cook with my hands, eyes and heart, not just the recipe. Some of her recipes are now mine, and I strive for her light touch and to know when to stop mixing! There are rules to follow to produce a good sponge cake: egg temperature, glass bowls and sifted flour, to name a few. Producing a great sponge cake is about these rules and your senses. A successful sponge cake is a reward for the taste buds and a triumph for the cook.

SERVES 12

315 g (11 oz) caster (superfine) sugar, plus extra to coat the tin

235 g (8½ oz) plain (all-purpose) flour, plus extra to coat the tin

9 g ¼ oz baking powder

100 g (3½ oz) butter, plus extra for greasing

6 eggs (330 g), at room temperature

300 g (10½ oz) Rhubarb and lemon myrtle jam (see page 251)

400 ml (13½ fl oz) cream, whipped

icing sugar, for dusting

1. Preheat the oven to 180°C (360°F) and grease and line two 20 cm (8 in) cake tins.

2. Place a little sugar on the inside edge of the cake tin and roll it around the rim to evenly coat the edge. Pour the excess into the other tin and repeat the process, adding more sugar if needed. Discard any remaining sugar. Repeat the process with flour to coat each tin.

3. Sift the flour and baking powder three times. Melt the butter with 3 teaspoons of water in a small pot over a low heat.

4. Whisk the eggs in a medium bowl until they begin to turn pale and foamy. Add the sugar a third at a time, whisking after each addition. Once thick, pale and creamy, gently but quickly fold the flour and butter into the eggs, retaining as much air as possible. Divide the mixture between the tins and quickly place them in the oven. The quicker this process happens, the more air will remain in the batter. Bake for 30 minutes, or until the sponges spring back when gently pressed on the surface.

5. Remove the tins from the oven and immediately invert the cakes onto a rack covered with a tea towel to cool completely.

6. Cut the cakes in half horizontally. On three of the layers, spread a thin layer of jam across the surface and top the jam with a layer of whipped cream. Stack the dressed cakes, top with the undressed sponge and dust with a little icing sugar.

RHUBARB AND LEMON MYRTLE JAM

Imagine how much abundant ripe produce jam factories have prevented from going to landfill; however, overcooked fruit loaded with refined sugar is not my idea of a good time, so I like to make my own jam to limit the amount of sugar used. Sugar is the preserver in jam, and the ripeness of the fruit determines how much sugar to use. Making jam with ripe fruit reduces the amount of sugar and the cooking time. The jam will have a brighter flavour too. Add acid towards the end of the cooking process in the form of orange, lemon or lime juice to balance the sweetness. Seal the jam hot for an extended shelf life.

WHAT YOU'LL NEED
- sterilised jars (see page 21)

1.4 kg (3 lb 1 oz) rhubarb, trimmed and cut into 6 cm (2½ in) lengths

---

750 g (1 lb 11 oz) caster (superfine) sugar

---

zest and juice of 1 orange

---

3 pinches ground lemon myrtle

---

1. Cook the rhubarb, sugar and orange zest and juice in a covered pot over a medium heat for 5 minutes to soften the rhubarb and dissolve the sugar.

2. Uncover and cook for a further 30–40 minutes, until thick and glossy. Test the jam is ready by placing a teaspoon of the rhubarb onto a cold plate and tilting the plate – when the jam holds together and doesn't slide down the plate, it's ready.

3. Add the lemon myrtle and stir it through. Pour the hot jam into sterilised jars and seal the jars. Cool completely at room temperature. The jam will last up to 12 months. Refrigerate after opening.

29

Whole orange parfait with citrus-butter sauce

If it ain't frozen, it's not dessert. Not entirely true but a sweet, creamy frozen parfait is a delight. Best of all, you don't need an ice-cream machine to achieve the silkiness we all love from a frozen treat. This parfait is flavoured with puree made from whole oranges, but you can substitute them with any seasonal fruit. To prevent the parfait from becoming icy, be sure to let all the steam escape when you're cooling the orange puree.

SERVES 6-8

8 egg yolks

1 tablespoon lemon juice

250 g (9 oz) caster (superfine) sugar

1 vanilla bean, split and seeds scraped

200 g (7 oz) Orange puree (see page 259), cooled

250 g (9 oz) crème fraiche

200 g (7 oz) cream, whipped

1 × quantity Citrus–butter sauce (see page 259), to serve

1 × quantity Candied fennel seeds (see page 259), to serve

1. Grease and line a 20 × 12 cm (8 × 4¾ in) loaf tin and set aside in the freezer.

2. Whisk the yolks, sugar and lemon juice in a medium heatproof bowl. Place the bowl over a simmering pot of water, making sure the bowl isn't touching the water. Cook, continually whisking, for 5 minutes, or until the mixture is pale and thick.

3. Remove the bowl from the heat, add the vanilla and continue to whisk to cool slightly. Gently fold in the orange puree, then the crème fraiche. Fold in the whipped cream and pour the mixture into the prepared tin. Freeze overnight.

4. Turn the frozen parfait out onto a piece of baking paper on a chopping board. Cut into portions and serve scattered with candied fennel seeds and citrus–butter sauce to the side.

ORANGE PUREE

2 oranges

1. Place the whole oranges in a pot and cover with water. Bring to the boil and simmer for 40 minutes, or until the oranges are soft and cooked through. Drain.

2. Blend the oranges in a food processor until smooth, then set aside to cool completely, allowing the steam to escape.

3. Store in the fridge in an airtight container for 2 weeks or in the freezer for up to 3 months.

CITRUS-BUTTER SAUCE

zest and juice of 5 oranges

300 g (10½ oz/1¼ cups) caster (superfine) sugar

100 g (3½ oz) cold butter, diced

1. Place the orange zest and juice and the sugar in a pot and bring to a simmer over a medium–low heat for 15–20 minutes, or until the liquid has reduced and begins to thicken.

2. Whisk the cold butter into the syrup piece by piece until it emulsifies. Remove the pot from the heat and stir it occasionally as it cools. The sauce will keep for 2 weeks in an airtight container in the fridge.

CANDIED FENNEL SEEDS

WHAT YOU'LL NEED
• thermometer

2½ tablespoons fennel seeds

80 g (2¾ oz/⅓ cup) caster (superfine) sugar

3½ tablespoons poppy seeds

1. Toast the fennel seeds in a dry frying pan over a medium heat until fragrant.

2. In a small pot, bring the sugar and 4 tablespoons of water to 110°C (230°F). Add the fennel seeds and poppy seeds and stir until the sugar crystallises and coats the seeds. Remove from the heat and cool completely on a tray or a plate. The seeds can be stored in a container for up to 12 months.

Whole orange parfait with citrus–butter sauce

30

Honey–miso caramel

Miso adds seasoning and body to an array of dishes, and paired with honey it tastes similar to salted caramel. In this recipe, toasted seeds and nuts are bound together with caramelised honey for a hybrid toffee–seedy petit four.

MAKES 20 PIECES

60 g (2 oz/⅓ cup) pepitas (pumpkin seeds)

15 g (½ oz/2 tablespoons) sesame seeds

50 g (1¾ oz/⅓ cup) sunflower seeds

80 g (2¾ oz/½ cup) macadamia nuts

85 g (3 oz/½ cup) cashew nuts

420 g (15 oz/1 cup) honey

zest of 1 orange

2 tablespoons Miso (see recipe opposite), or 1 tablespoon store-bought miso

1. Preheat the oven to 170°C (340°F).

2. Lay the seeds on one tray and the nuts on another and bake both trays for 12–15 minutes, or until the seeds and nuts are golden. The nuts will take slightly longer. Cool completely.

3. Roughly chop the nuts in half and combine them with the seeds. Grease a 20 × 20 cm (8 × 8 in) baking tray and line it with baking paper.

4. Heat the honey to 160°C (320°F) in a tall, medium saucepan over a low–medium heat. The honey will bubble and foam.

5. Remove it from the heat and stir through the orange zest and miso. Stir in the seeds and nuts, then pour the mix onto the lined tray to cool completely.

6. Once cool, cut the caramel into squares using a sharp knife. The caramel can be stored in an airtight container for 4 weeks, or freeze it for a longer shelf life and a firmer texture for up to 3 months.

MISO

Seems crazy now, but for a long time, making miso appeared exotic and a great mystery to me. The search for clear and accurate information sent me down a rabbit hole, and 'How do you make miso?' soon became 'What the hell is koji?'. I stumbled my way through making my first batch of soy bean miso plagued with doubt, and I was too scared to taste it, fearing I would poison myself. It was a chance meeting with Japanese food specialist Nancy Singleton Hachisu that sent me on the right track. She reassured me the look and taste were normal and I was doing a good job. Although the Western world is becoming familiar with miso, I appreciated Nancy's gift of confidence to persist with this historic and traditional form of fermentation. This recipe uses 50 per cent koji rice and 12 per cent salt to the weight of soy beans (see page 21).

WHAT YOU'LL NEED
• sterilised jar (see page 21) or miso crock

750 g (1 lb 11 oz) Koji rice
1.4 kg (3 lb 1 oz) dry organic soy beans, soaked overnight
260 g (9 oz) fine salt
1 teaspoon extra-fine salt

1. Drain the beans and add them to a large pot of water. Bring them to a simmer over a medium heat and cook for 30–35 minutes, or until completely tender. Drain, retaining a small amount of the cooking liquid.

2. Place the beans into a large bowl and when cool enough to handle, with gloved hands squeeze to roughly break up approximately two-thirds of the beans.

3. Add the koji rice and fine salt and mix to combine. The texture of the unfermented miso should be firm but malleable. If it feels dry add some of the cooking liquid to soften.

4. Firmly pack the miso into the sterilised jar or crock, making sure there are no air bubbles, and sprinkle the extra-fine salt over the surface of the paste. Cut a circle of baking paper slightly bigger than the surface of the miso and press it flush with the surface of the miso to cover. Cover the jar with a lid.

5. Place the miso in a cool dark environment for a minimum of 7 months and up 2 years to ferment. The miso is ready when it doesn't taste like alcohol but more floral and earthy. Once fermented the miso can be blended into a paste or left textured and stored in a sterilised jar or in the fridge.

Acknowledgements

Massive thank you to Mum. I couldn't have written this book and gotten through many challenging times without you and your unwavering support. I really appreciate your honesty, how you challenge and bring out the best in me. I think my writing has gotten better thanks to you!

Dad, thank you for pushing me to learn new skills and believe in my passion. You always show interest in what I do and provide a different perspective.

To my aunty Robyn, thank you for letting me mess up your kitchen, for taking me to the market and supporting my dream of becoming a chef.

Matt Stone, my once partner and forever friend. Thank you for always having my back, believing in me and creating with me. You have given me so much confidence to never falter from my beliefs.

Joost and Jennie Bakker, futurefoodsystem was an extremely clarifying time. Thank you for the opportunity, for taking the risk and for being so passionate. Not just for me, but for the whole planet. I'm not sure I will ever have such an intense learning experience again. I loved it and I am forever grateful.

Lousie Daily, the rock, the brain and the muscle. You are an absolute powerhouse of a human. I don't know how I would have done this without you, especially whilst opening a restaurant and starting a pie company together! I am so lucky to have you in my life. Thank you for everything you are and do.

David Osgood, thank you for being so patient and understanding. You're the ultimate in so many ways. Love you.

To Roxy Ryan, Michael Harry, Antonietta Anello, Daniel New, Mark Roper, Lee Blaylock and the whole Hardie Grant team. It has been a dream to write a book and working with such a creative passionate team has been an incredible experience. Thank you!!

And lastly to my food-tech teachers at high school – Sonja, Jennifer Wright and Mrs Smith the OG's. Thanks for letting me use the kitchens during lunch time.

Index

A

aged fenugreek 39

aioli

aioli sauce 135

Barramundi and sorghum tostadas with pickled jalapeños and coriander seeds 78

Smoke d trout with celeriac and spring onion remoulade 131

almonds

Fried sardines with roasted almonds, skordalia and parsley salad 156

avocado

Avocado salsa with parsley-seed dressing and eggs on toast 116

B

bacon

Brussels sprouts and bacon with mushroom XO 208

curing and smoking bacon 210

baking with precision 248

Bakker, Joost 11, 26, 30, 130

barramundi

Barramundi and sorghum tostadas with pickled jalapeños and coriander seeds 78

Barrett, Jo

background 18, 25–6

early influences 25–6

beans

fermented beans 102, 105

Zucchini and fermented beans rice cakes 99–105

besan flour

batter 102

Sprout balls with cashew and fenugreek 33–9

bone broth 58, 146-7

bottling vegetables 181

brine 58, 105

broccoli

Broccoli, buckwheat and seaweed salad 119–25

brown rice flour batter 102

brussels sprouts

Brussels sprouts and bacon with mushroom XO 205–11

buckwheat

Broccoli, buckwheat and seaweed salad 119–23

buckwheat noodles 151

Rooster broth with buckwheat noodles and pickled mushrooms 145–151

Ultimate seed mix 213–16

bullhorn pepper

marinated vegetable dressing 162

preserved vegetables 165

butter

churning and flavouring 59

compound butter 59

cultured butter 60

Roasted marrow bones with compound butter on sourdough 55–65

button mushrooms

Glazed mushroom skewers 41–47

C

cabbage

Sauerkraut soup with fromage blanc 137–43

caccio ricotta 243

calculations and recipes 17

capers

Stuffed rainbow chard with olives, capers and preserved lemon in tomato sugo 175–181

cashews

cashew and fenugreek cream 39

cashew cream 195

Honey-miso caramel 261–65

Sprout balls with cashew and fenugreek 33–9

celeriac

Smoked trout with celeriac and spring onion remoulade 127–35

charcuterie 97, 210

chard

Stuffed rainbow chard with olives, capers and preserved lemon in tomato sugo 175–181

cheese making 143, 243

chicken

rooster bone broth 149

Rooster broth with buckwheat noodles and pickled mushrooms 145–151

chickpeas

chickpea flour batter 102

Sprout risotto 191–95

sprouting pulses and grains 39

chilli

Barramundi and sorghum tostadas with pickled jalapeños and coriander seeds 75–81

chilli oil 73

fermented chilli 209

'nduja 91–97

pickled jalapeños 79

Stuffed potato cakes with tomato-chilli relish 83–9

tomato-chilli relish 89

Yabbie dumplings with nasturtium and chilli oil 67–73

citrus

citrus-butter sauce 259

citrus oil 233

Layered lemon with granita, honey and yuzu curd 227–33

lemon granita 230, 232

orange puree 256, 259

Whole orange parfait with citrus-butter sauce 253–9

preserved lemons 181

Stuffed rainbow chard with olives, capers and preserved lemon in tomato sugo 173 yuzu curd 232

yuzu oil 232

citrus-butter sauce 259

citrus oil 232-3

compound butter 59

confit garlic 135

coriander

Barramundi and sorghum tostadas with pickled jalapeños and coriander seeds 75–81

cultured butter 60

cumin

cumin spice mix 52

Cumin wallaby skewers with garlicsauce 49–53

D

diced dressing

Broccoli, buckwheat and seaweed salad 119–25

diced dressing 125

E

eggs

aioli sauce 135

Avocado salsa with parsley-seed dressing and eggs on toast 113–17

F

fennel

candied fennel seeds 259

fennel salad 162

Murray cod with fennel salad and marinated vegetable dressing 159–65

Whole orange parfait with citrus-butter sauce 253–9

fenugreek

cashew and fenugreek cream 39

Sprout balls with cashew and fenugreek 33–9

fermenting foods 47, 143, 189, 265

beans 105

chilli 209

red peppers 189

fish

Barramundi and sorghum tostadas with pickled jalapeños and coriander seeds 75–81

Fried sardines with roasted almonds, skordalia and parsley salad 153–7

Murray cod with fennel salad and marinated vegetable dressing 159–65

Smoked trout with celeriac and spring onion remoulade 127–35

flaxseeds

Ultimate seed mix 213–17

flour

Freshly milled flatbread with 'nduja and sweet onion 91–7

milling grains at home 97

freezing foods 232, 256

Fried sardines with roasted almonds, skordalia and parsley salad 153–7

fromage blanc

making fromage blanc 143

Sauerkraut soup with fromage blanc 137–43

futurefoodsystem 11, 18

G

galette pastry 241

Garden bread 107–11

garlic

confit garlic 135

garlic yoghurt 52

Glazed mushroom skewers 41–47

gluten free cooking 14, 110

grain milling 97

grains

Sprout risotto 191–95

sprouting grains and pulses 39

grapeseed oil 18

green coriander seeds 79

Greenhouse project 11

H

Hachisu, Nancy Singleton 265

hemp seeds

Ultimate seed mix 213–16

honey

honey-cooked quinces 225

Honey-miso caramel 261–65

Tigernut cake with preserved quince 219–25

J

jalapeños

Barramundi and sorghum tostadas with pickled jalapeños and coriander seeds 75–81

pickled jalapeños 79

(*See also* chilli)

K

king oyster mushrooms

Glazed mushroom skewers 41–47

kitchen necessities 22

koji rice 47

miso 265

koji spores 47

L

Layered lemon with granita, honey and yuzu curd 227–33

lemon granita 232

lemon myrtle

Sponge cake with rhubarb and lemon myrtle jam 245–51

lemons

Layered lemon with granita, honey and yuzu curd 227–33

lemon granita 232

preserved lemons 181

Stuffed rainbow chard with olives, capers and preserved lemon in tomato sugo 175–181

lentils

Sprout balls with cashew and fenugreek 33–9

Sprout risotto 191–95

sprouting pulses and grains 39

linseed

Ultimate seed mix 213–16

M

macadamia nuts

Broccoli, buckwheat and seaweed salad 119–25

Honey-miso caramel 261–65

macadamia milk 125

macadamia pesto 203

maize

Garden bread 107–11

marinated vegetable dressing 162

meat

Cumin wallaby skewers with garlic sauce 49–53

Roasted marrow bones with compound butter on sourdough 55–65

Rooster broth with buckwheat noodles and pickled mushrooms 145–51

Venison and red wine pie 167–73

milling grains 97

miso
    Honey-miso caramel 261–65
    making miso 265
mung beans
    Sprout balls with cashew
      and fenugreek 33–9
    Sprout risotto 191–95
    sprouting pulses and grains 39
Murray cod with fennel salad
  and marinated vegetable
  dressing 159–65
mushrooms
    Brussels sprouts and bacon
      with mushroom XO 205–11
    Glazed mushroom skewers 41–47
    mushroom garum 47
    mushroom glaze 44
    mushroom XO 209
    pickled mushrooms 149
    Rooster broth with buckwheat
      noodles and pickled
      mushrooms 145–9

N
nasturtium leaves
    Yabbie dumplings with
      nasturtium and chilli oil 67–73
'nduja
    Freshly milled flatbread with
      'nduja and sweet onion 91–97
    'nduja sausage spread 97
nixtamalisation 80
noodle making 151
nut creams 39, 195
nut milk 125
nutrients 30

O
olive oil 22
olives
    Stuffed rainbow chard with
      olives, capers and preserved
      lemon in tomato sugo 175–9
oranges
    citrus-butter sauce 259
    orange puree 259
    Whole orange parfait with
      citrus-butter sauce 253–9

P
pantry staples 31
parfait making 256
Whole orange parfait with
  citrus-butter sauce 253–9

parsley
    Avocado salsa with parsley-seed
      dressing and eggs on toast 113–17
    Fried sardines with roasted
      almonds, skordalia and
      parsley salad 153–57
    herb flower and seed oil 117
    parsley salad 156
    parsley-seed dressing 117
pasta
    Red pepper pasta 183–9
    rye pasta 189
pastry
    galette pastry 241
    Plum galette with caccio
      ricotta 235–43
    rough puff pastry 173
    Venison and red wine pie 167–73
pepitas
    Honey-miso caramel 261–65
    Ultimate seed mix 213–16
peppers
    fermented red peppers 189
    marinated vegetable dressing 162
    Red pepper pasta 183–9
pesto
    macadamia pesto 203
    Roast potatoes with
      macadamia pesto 197–203
pickling foods
    jalapeños 79
    mushrooms 149
pie making 170–73
plums
    bottled plums 241
    Plum galette with caccio
      ricotta 235–43
polenta
    Garden bread 107–11
pork
    'nduja 91–97
potato
    Fried sardines with roasted
      almonds, skordalia and
      parsley salad 153–7
    Roast potatoes with
      macadamia pesto 197–203
    skordalia 156
    Stuffed potato cakes with
      tomato-chilli relish 83–9
poultry
    rooster bone broth 149
    Rooster broth with buckwheat
      noodles and pickled
      mushrooms 145–11

preserving food 31
    in alcohol 241
    in honey 225
    lemons 181
    in oil 73, 117, 165, 203, 209, 233
    in oil and vinegar 125
    as a relish 89
    with salt 181, 210
    with smoke 132
    with sugar 251
    vegetables 165, 181
    in vinegar 39
puff pastry 173
pulses
    Sprout risotto 191–95
    sprouting pulses and
      grains 39
pumpkin
    Garden bread 107–11
    puree 111
pumpkin seeds
    Honey-miso caramel 261–65
    Ultimate seed mix 213–16
puy lentils
    Sprout balls with cashew
      and fenugreek 33–9
    Sprout risotto 191–95
    sprouting pulses and
      grains 39

Q
quinces
    honey-cooked quinces 225
    Tigernut cake with preserved
      quince 219–25

R
rainbow chard
    Stuffed rainbow chard with
      olives, capers and preserved
      lemon in tomato sugo 175–11
Red pepper pasta 183–9
red wine vinegar 165
rhubarb
    rhubarb and lemon myrtle
      jam 251
    Sponge cake with rhubarb and
      lemon myrtle jam 245–51
rice
    Sprout risotto 191–95
    sprouting pulses and grains 39
    Stuffed rainbow chard with
      olives, capers and preserved
      lemon in tomato sugo 175–181

ricotta
Plum galette with caccio
ricotta 235–43
risotto
Sprout risotto 191–95
Roast potatoes with
macadamia pesto 197–203
rooster
rooster bone broth 149
Rooster broth with buckwheat
noodles and pickled
mushrooms 145–151
rye pasta 189

S
salt 22
brine 58
curing 210
sardines
Fried sardines with roasted
almonds, skordalia and
parsley salad 153–7
sauerkraut
Sauerkraut soup with
fromage blanc 137–43
seaweed
Broccoli, buckwheat and
seaweed salad 119–25
sesame seeds
Honey-miso caramel 261–65
Ultimate seed mix 213–16
shiitake mushrooms
Glazed mushroom skewers 41–47
silverbeet
Stuffed potato cakes with
tomato-chilli relish 83–9
skordalia 156
Smoked trout with celeriac and
spring onion remoulade 127–35
smoking and curing trout 132
smoking meats 210
sorghum
Barramundi and sorghum
tostadas with pickled jalapeños
and coriander seeds 75–10
sorghum tostadas 80
sourdough
Avocado salsa with
parsley-seed dressing
and eggs on toast 113–17
baking method 65
levain feed 62
starter 62

soy beans
miso 265
spices
Cumin wallaby skewers
with garlic sauce 49–53
spinach puree 194
Sponge cake with rhubarb and
lemon myrtle jam 245–251
sprouts
Sprout balls with cashew
and fenugreek 33–9
Sprout risotto 191–95
sprouting pulses and
grains 39
sterilising equipment 21
Stone, Matt 26, 30, 208
Stuffed potato cakes with
tomato-chilli relish 83–9
Stuffed rainbow chard with
olives, capers and preserved
lemon in tomato sugo 175–181
sugar 22
sunflower seeds
Honey-miso caramel 261–65
sustainable eating 21–22, 25

T
tigernuts
Tigernut cake with preserved
quince 219–25
tomato
marinated vegetable
dressing 162
Stuffed potato cakes with
tomato-chilli relish 83–9
Stuffed rainbow chard with
olives, capers and preserved
lemon in tomato sugo 175–181
tomato-chilli relish 89, 102
tomato sugo 181
Venison and red wine pie 167–73
trout
Smoked trout with
celeriac and spring onion
remoulade 127–35
smoking and curing trout 132

U
Ultimate seed mix 213–16

V
vegan cooking 30
vegetables
preserved vegetables 165, 181

venison
Venison and red wine pie 167–73
vinegar 18
making vinegar 165
red wine vinegar 165

W
wakame flakes
Broccoli, buckwheat and
seaweed salad 119–25
wallaby
Cumin wallaby skewers with
garlic sauce 49–53
waste 14–15
Wood, Colin 143

Y
yabbies
Yabbie dumplings with
nasturtium and chilli oil 67–73
yoghurt
Cumin wallaby skewers
with garlic sauce 49–53
making yoghurt 53
yuzu
Layered lemon with granita,
honey and yuzu curd 227–33
yuzu curd 232
yuzu oil 233

Z
zero waste 18, 28, 30
zucchini
Zucchini and fermented beans
rice cakes 99–105

Published in 2023 by Hardie Grant Books, an imprint of Hardie Grant Publishing

Hardie Grant Books (Melbourne)
Wurundjeri Country
Building 1, 658 Church Street
Richmond, Victoria 3121

Hardie Grant Books (London)
5th & 6th Floors
52–54 Southwark Street
London SE1 1UN

hardiegrant.com/books

Hardie Grant acknowledges the Traditional Owners of the Country on which we work, the Wurundjeri People of the Kulin Nation and the Gadigal People of the Eora Nation, and recognises their continuing connection to the land, waters and culture. We pay our respects to their Elders past and present.

 A catalogue record for this book is available from the National Library of Australia

Sustain
ISBN 978 1 74379 884 3

10 9 8 7 6 5 4 3 2 1

Publisher: Michael Harry
Project Editor: Antonietta Anello
Editor: Helena Holmgren
Design Manager: Kristin Thomas
Designer: Daniel New
Typsetters: Hannah Schubert and Daniel New
Photographer: Mark Roper
Stylist: Lee Blaylock
Chef: Louise Daily
Production Manager: Todd Rechner
Production Coordinator: Jessica Harvie

Colour reproduction by Splitting Image Colour Studio
Printed in China by Leo Paper Products LTD.

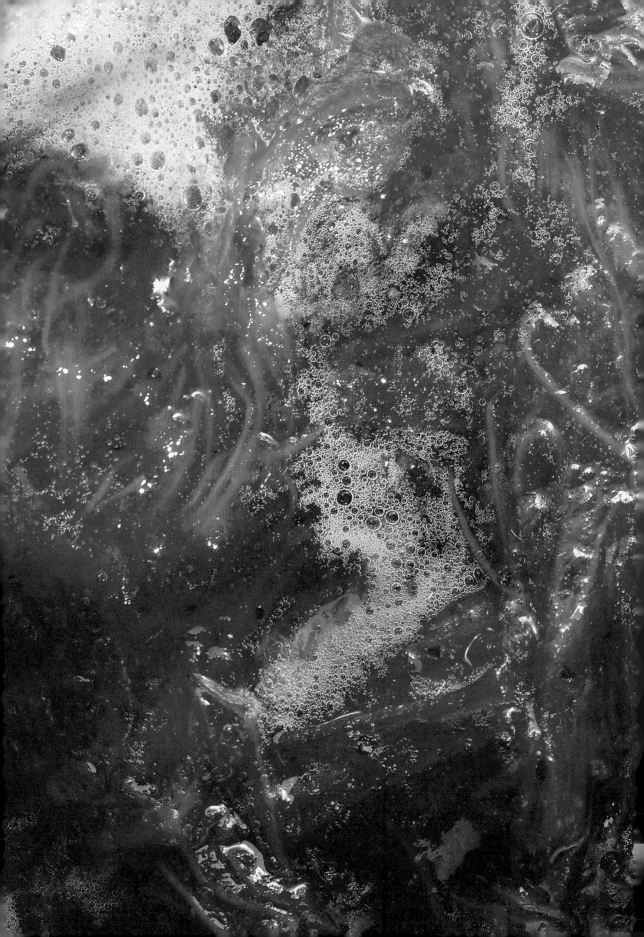